Get Your Ex Back

The Ultimate Guide to Becoming Their Obsession

(The Ultimate Guide on How to Get Your Ex Back Fast and Keep Your Lover Forever)

Tyrone Spinelli

Published By **Phil Dawson**

Tyrone Spinelli

All Rights Reserved

Get Your Ex Back: The Ultimate Guide to Becoming Their Obsession (The Ultimate Guide on How to Get Your Ex Back Fast and Keep Your Lover Forever)

ISBN 978-1-7776902-5-0

No part of this guidebook shall be reproduced in any form without permission in writing from the publisher except in the case of brief quotations embodied in critical articles or reviews.

Legal & Disclaimer

The information contained in this book is not designed to replace or take the place of any form of medicine or professional medical advice. The information in this book has been provided for educational & entertainment purposes only.

The information contained in this book has been compiled from sources deemed reliable, and it is accurate to the best of the Author's knowledge; however, the Author cannot guarantee its accuracy and validity and cannot be held liable for any errors or omissions. Changes are periodically made to this book. You must consult your doctor or get professional medical advice before using any of the suggested remedies, techniques, or information in this book.

Upon using the information contained in this book, you agree to hold harmless the Author from and against any damages, costs, and expenses, including any legal fees potentially resulting from the application of any of the information provided by this guide. This disclaimer applies to any damages or injury caused by the use and application, whether directly or indirectly, of any advice or information presented, whether for breach of contract, tort, negligence, personal injury, criminal intent, or under any other cause of action.

You agree to accept all risks of using the information presented inside this book. You need to consult a professional medical practitioner in order to ensure you are both able and healthy enough to participate in this program.

Table Of Contents

Chapter 1: Why You Should Definitely Not Get Back With Your Ex 1

Chapter 2: What Makes An Ex Come Back 15

Chapter 3: Signs You Ought To Ponder ... 27

Chapter 4: Powerful Prayers To Get Your Ex Back 37

Chapter 5: Battles Of Reuniting Together 44

Chapter 6: Get Back With A Previous Sweetheart 50

Chapter 7: Why Do We Want To Recover What Has Been Lost? 71

Chapter 8: The Psychology Behind Breakups 85

Chapter 9: Demystifying Romantic Love . 97

Chapter 10: Personal Reconstruction ... 107

Chapter 11: Communication And Its Secrets And Techniques And Strategies 117

Chapter 12: Ancient Love Rituals 130

Chapter 13: Neuroscience Of Love 143

Chapter 14: Understanding The Break Up
.... 150

Chapter 15: Rebuilding Trust 164

Chapter 16: Facing Challenges 175

Chapter 1: Why You Should Definitely Not Get Back With Your Ex

The folks that want to repair a courting should painstakingly take a look at assuming this is smart that large different who unloaded you may as however be a similar person. The reasons you parted strategies with any person may additionally anyways flip out as predicted. Or but you may sincerely be deliberating accommodating for some unacceptable reasons.

This pocket e book will check out why you may be feeling you need to get yet again at the side of your ex, four justifications for why rejoining may be an errors.

Why You're Having this have an effect on

After you encountered a dating separation, you in all likelihood felt disheartened, miserable and had near domestic ache. You may likely've even emerged as discouraged.

As time elapsed, you probably tracked down strategies of transferring past that man or woman in the long run cited it wasn't working. Or then again you understood the 2 humans want to want the connection. Assuming that your ex reduce it off or you chop off the friendship, both of you have been no longer in and now not the use of a reservations.

Notwithstanding the ones motives, you might be re-questioning yourself. It's plausible you undergo in mind you are though infatuated alongside your ex and are ruminating over the separation. Perhaps you have got been helped to bear in mind the thrilled times you spent collectively and notion decrease once more with the aid of searching at photos in your phone. You saw your ex, recalled the great times, and presently view the reference to rose-hued glasses.

Additionally, Assuming you in fact see your ex as extremely attractive and you come to be accepting they may be desired for investigating you, that would simply play into your yearning to accompany that person.

Reasons Rejoining May Be an Error

Couples cut up up on motive. Certain human beings mistake missing any man or woman for trying to reunite. The following are four warnings that display reviving your sentiment can be a poorly conceived notion.

Loss of Trust

Suppose your ex cheated and you pardoned them. Pardoning lets in the individual to push ahead. But since you stayed doubtful even after the superiority and at in reality no point ever believed your ex within the destiny, you became separated. You have been no longer capable of share your personal worries or fears; you were unable to open up and be open to them.

While couples can reconstruct don't forget in their connections, real closeness dreams accept as true with as its popularity quo. You want to be with a sympathetic, accomplice, someone you receive as actual with who likewise confides in you.

Issues With Correspondence

Correspondence encourages affiliation. On the off threat that your ex hides subjects faraway from simple view, saved faraway from difficult discussions or becomes forceful and hollered, recognize that you gain an accomplice who thinks frequently approximately you and imparts consciously.

While all connections have conflicts, contending damagingly can harm connections. Checking in with every exclusive on unremarkable, calculated subjects, however on greater profound problems is solid in an organization.

On the off danger that you or your ex-companion have not turn out to be better communicators, those issues can without a doubt have an effect on a revived courting.

Disarray Among Desire and Love

In the occasion that precise the assessment among preference and love, really take into account a 2d: Do your memories of your times collectively spin round amazing sex is difficult? Sexual technology is about actual fascination and not absolutely about a close-by profound association.

however, consolidates sexual yearning and sexual encounters with a profound, getting through bond.

While it is able to appear like difficult to symbolize love, it's miles conceivable. Love can be described as a conscious, devoted, and profound near home connection. Researchers have long past above and beyond.

Leading a notably massive, intercultural evaluation in a modern report throughout 25 international locations, logical examination proof confirmed that three important components of affection describe heartfelt connections: closeness, enthusiasm, and responsibility.

While those components aren't normally present simultaneously or further seeing a person, research indicates those are crucial factors of affection.

Absence of companionship

As indicated via The Gottman Establishment, fellowship is important to the essentialness of a drawn out dating. However the movement snap shots basically painting outsiders experiencing passionate feelings for, as consistent with logical exam exposed in a cutting-edge report, maximum couples begin as partners.

WHEN YOU SHOULD NOT TO GET BACK WITH YOUR EX

Every scenario varies from one man or woman to some other, however there are times while getting back collectively in conjunction with your ex sooner or later in the end finally ends up being incomprehensible or perhaps profoundly horrendous.

Prior to continuing, we sincerely want to intensify that there are instances at the same time as you need to not reunite with an ex, for any motive. These embody:

Your ex became inwardly, loudly, or truly risky

They are presently seeing a few different person

Your ex knowledgeable you straightforwardly that the man or woman isn't always open for compromise, no matter what you do

They are in a situation of sorrow, outrage, or franticness

You will encounter hopeless harm on your rate variety, vocation, and prosperity on the off chance which you reunite with an ex

These are the number one justifications for why getting decrease again with an ex would possibly in no way be clever. These occurrences will possibly object to extra harm than some detail else if you come what may took place to choose out to reunite in conjunction with your ex.

On the off chance which you cannot connect to any of the matters on that rundown, but, you may hold to the following phase of this thing.

WHY DO I WANT TO GET BACK WITH MY EX, AND IS IT EVEN WORTH THE EFFORT?

Indeed, even numerous years after the detachment, the attention of your ex can make you start dreaming about being collectively over again, or if no longer some thing else start feeling a wistfulness of some kind or another. For numerous reasons you haven't grieved the connection but, wherein it counts you're certainly feeling a few element for this character.

It couldn't genuinely be love but there are such infinite beautiful recollections that make you contemplate how remarkable you felt collectively, and also you truly have no choice to land up with regrets.

Assuming you experience which you're the primary man or woman who has at any factor felt like this, don't be mindless. Out of the relative multitude of individuals I mentor after a separation that befell quite some time inside the past, a large a part of them revel in the same way you do! Many people need to be with their ex over again due to each considered certainly certainly one of their memories.

So how might also moreover you're making revel in of the manner that high-quality people can swiftly preserve on on the equal time as you definitely can not get your ex as far away from you as feasible?

There are manifestly many motives that could make enjoy of why you actually need to be near them no matter the partition. Nonetheless, your affectionate sentiments aren't normally the possible aim, irrespective of whether or not or no longer they may be no longer a few element to dismiss.

It's crucial to pay attention to that that is simply not a simple condition to be in at the grounds that you have such countless inquiries, you do no longer understand whether or not or no longer it's far in reality clever to try to get decrease lower back together together together with your ex.

Choosing to try to reunite a long time after the branch is not any piece of cake, so it's miles critical to provide an cause of the reasons for the craving so you can in the end sort out the maximum pleasant technique.

Individuals often query me, "Willis Gottman, for what motive should I want to get decrease lower back with my ex after the quantity they harm me?" It's a few issue however a easy inquiry to respond to in moderate of the fact that each courting is quite novel.

For this cause I suggest perusing this e-book, "How to Get Your Ex Back" or putting in an association for a training assembly with the motive that you may make the maximum of man or woman route.

By and by using, you should realize that because of my revel in as a mentor, and a teacher, I certainly have had the selection to determine the 5 motives we see maximum often in human beings.

For what purpose could probably I want to get back with my ex? Find 2 "terrific" motivations inside the lower back of why!

No, your ex hasn't positioned a revile on you of a few type on the off danger which you're in truth thinking about them months or maybe a long term after the separation! I will provide you with some clarifications behind this peculiarity to be able to doubtlessly relate on your ongoing scenario.

In your eyes, it might be tremendous that you need your ex lower back because you're still enamored or in slight of the reality which you lament a choice made too hurriedly. Assuming you're sporting out in the next splendor, make sure that you're not encountering profound reliance or that you're glorifying your ex.

The Fundamental clarification

I love my ex and I can not envision my existence without them.

Starting from the start of this ebook I've momentarily addressed the essential purpose for what purpose you will need your ex once more, however I have now not lengthy past as a substitute far into detail concerning the trouble.

It's approximately Affection! It's generally anticipated to be the most coherent clarification but however it is the most sensitive because of the truth that it's far precarious even as you accept as true with it is the precept issue directing you! In truth there are various little clarifications but you have got been dazed and do not see one in all a kind reasons for the reason that your feelings are dominating.

This could no longer suggest which you're now not feeling any adoration but as an opportunity almost truly, you're fact be suggested feeling near domestic reliance. Not that is all terrible on the grounds that in fact, you honestly want to find an equilibrium yet again.

So absolutely, manifestly you're thinking, "I certainly love my ex," and also you lament the aggregate-u.S.A.That bring about the separation. It's completely common which you'd need to start another time and adjust a sturdy dating in that you ensure you regret absolutely not anything and revel in happy.

You've understood how excellent they are a number one a part of your life and currently it is the correct time to reveal them the better than ever You! (Sensibly talking, glaringly…)

I lament the separation!

Here, we aren't discussing the people that had been stated a very last farewell to; we are discussing individuals that settled on the choice to move away. However, with time, that they had understood that their ex grow to be The One. You can truely lighten up at the off threat which you're in this present circumstance too, thinking about that irrespective of whether or not or now not you pick out to cut up it is viable to get another time within the saddle to you!

All topics taken into consideration, really by no means allow regret assume command over your life because of the fact that this will ruin your lifestyles. An individual may moreover need to experience that that they had be more completely happy, that that that they had have the choice to have a far superior courting with each distinct man or woman, but assuming you are lamenting the shortfall of the person you had been offering your lifestyles to previously, you could not have the selection to maintain on inside the direction of a few element terrific.

Chapter 2: What Makes An Ex Come Back

Certainly, you want to reunite with them. Be that as it is able to, how can also want to an ex circulate lower back to you inside the event that it wasn't their concept? There are some motives, and proper proper right here are a number of them:

They leave out you

Since you separated does now not advocate that they probable won't miss having you in their life. You likely had a ton of extremely good instances collectively that they remember affectionately. They additionally might also moreover thoroughly leave out your friendship.

They absolutely love you

The truth that they really love you makes them feasible. Some adoration runs profound and may undergo for all time.

In this manner, probably they can not shake the manner that they without a doubt care deeply about you. They should have tried to hold on, however they proved unable.

They are lonely

Presently, this isn't the satisfactory justification in your ex to reunite with you. It's some thing but a fantastic one thru the usage of any stretch of the creativeness, as a depend of fact. Being forlorn is not motivation to head again to a relationship that wasn't walking. However, for a few humans, it is a justification for why they make it appear.

You have modified *or they've got*

Assuming which you were the person that devoted the maximum mistakes in the courting, possibly they anticipate you have got were given advanced and will permit you some different possibility. Or alternatively assuming they have been the individual that messed up, they have evolved and changed themselves.

They can't see a destiny without you

On the off hazard that they genuinely love and omit you, they probably may not have the option to examine their destiny without you.

They ought to anyways be especially appended to you and unfit to relinquish the fantasy that that they had of you being collectively for eternity

HOW LONG DOES IT TAKE FOR AN EX TO COME BACK

Nobody can at any component let you recognize how tough it has an inclination to be to transport beyond someone.

You realise you want your ex again, however you do now not have the foggiest concept what quantity of time it will require. Each person is particular, and their situation is as well.

At the thing at the same time as you are saying a very last farewell in your companion, you could need a while away, to count on and deal with the entire condition. The hardest issue is to emerge from the discouraging separation diploma and contemplate what to do straightaway.

You need to maintain on, but to get decrease back collectively with your ex, there is a ton of hard paintings that you really need to do earlier than you steer a degree that way.

We to start with activate you to thoroughly endure in thoughts your separation and decide out your sentiments. On the off hazard that, after plenty, you actually need to begin all once more in conjunction with your ex, then we're right here that will help you.

We realize you are traumatic to reunite and you still keep in mind what quantity of time it requires to get your ex once more. In any case, we exhort staying electricity. You cannot rush matters at the same time as others are likewise concerned.

Many humans will guarantee you that it will require 2-6 months to get your ex again. Be that as it can, we will undertake an exchange method.

We will talk diverse styles of separations and the speculative time it could take to get your ex once more.

Like we said formerly, each circumstance and all and sundry is precise, so it is basically now not feasible that we are capable of will let you recognise the appropriate time, but we are able to help you with information what amount of time it can require to get your ex lower lower back.

So right here are the top notch conditions and the manner prolonged it might take to get your separation

Shared separation

Shared separations are tremendous as is the risk of reuniting along aspect your ex. In the event that you each sense that the separation modified into some unacceptable desire, you can reunite in a rely type of moments. The most important time that it will require is the investment to decide your problems.

You need to triumph over each one of the problems earlier than you skip on, else there may be no usage in fixing matters up. Remove one month from your ex earlier than you undergo in mind reuniting.

Find an possibility to assess your profound country. Is it solid to say which you are prepared to reunite? Ask your self that. Do you think your ex may be keen on normally settling your troubles?

You really need to recognize the responses to the ones inquiries in advance than you push in advance. Whenever you have got eliminated a while after the separation, communicate together with your ex. Attempt to determine out their mind-set. When you find your sentiments, preserve in mind the time your ex will take to answer.

Try not to depend likely an excessive amount of on imagining that your ex will answer right away. Require essentially half of of a month's time no matter the fact that for that too. What's extra, there may be constantly a probability that your ex want to hold on and now not start once more with you. Then, at that aspect, you ought to bear in mind the time it's going to take at the way to searching for after your ex if you'll as an opportunity now not give up after the primary "no."

So it would require no an awful lot much less than months in the event that the separation come to be commonplace and genial and every of you need to reunite. Also, a few element like 4 months assuming you need your ex once more however your ex does now not apprehend.

At the issue while your ex Unloaded you

You commenced out the separation, but presently you need your ex again? This may be an irksome diploma because of the fact you're the person who harm your ex and presently you want to placed forth all the tries to win them decrease again.

In any case, earlier than that, you can require a threat to apprehend what triggered the separation and why you recollect you studied reuniting is truely smart. Ponder why you fell head over heels in your ex and why you separated.

Wonder why you unloaded your ex. Was your ex now not nice to you or could you are saying you have been too difficult to even consider handling? To start once more, you need to be honest with yourself.

Some of the time, while we are feeling desolate, we tragically keep in mind that we're feeling the lack of our ex, but that won't be valid.

At the point while you sell off your ex, you are out of nowhere stood up with a void. You have by myself time and you do now not have the foggiest idea what to do. You may additionally in reality need the employer of a person, no longer love essentially.

Try no longer to mistake depression for affection.

Get some margin to spend time collectively together with your companions. This will provide you with a notion of whether or not you're forlorn or nonetheless infatuated in conjunction with your ex. To talk together with your ex, even following a awesome night time day trip together along with your companions, then, at that issue, truly you bypass over your ex.

There is a few other danger which you leave out your ex because you pass over the eye and love. In the event that it is exquisite that, reconsider. Might it's miles stated that you are feeling the dearth of your ex or just the consideration?

Will you be in addition glad assuming you stand thrilled with every other person? You should recognize your dating earlier than you contemplate what quantity of time it's going to require to get your ex decrease back.

Whenever you have got concept about each one of the feasible outcomes, then, at that element, it can require no much much less than ninety days assuming you want your ex once more and that they need you decrease returned as properly. What's greater, 8 months at the off threat that you every do now not recognise and locating an opportunity to recognize your sentiments.

A ton will likewise rely upon how properly your ex solutions starting all yet again and checking out subjects.

Unpleasant Separation

Unpleasant separations are the hardest. They can devour apparently a big chunk of time to live to inform the story and determine the issues and some of the time the fulfillment price is 0.

Unpleasant separations seem at the same time as some factor outrageous takes place. Maybe your ex undermined you or went gaga for another character. On the off risk that your ex turn out to be harmful and fanatical, with a purpose to likewise result in a severe separation.

The inquiry proper proper right here is, might you are saying you're organized to swear off the entirety and cosmetics in conjunction with your ex irrespective of every in fact truly one of a few unacceptable matters they did to you? Can you carry on with a contented existence like this?

The inquiry proper right right here may not be the manner with the aid of manner of manner of which extended it'll take your ex to get decrease back, but how lengthy for you each to forgive and in no manner look once more.

This is exactly why we train a no touch period regarding basically a month to decide your head out. Harsh separations can go away you in strife. You want to discover a experience of contentment with your self and the times to recognize what come to be off-base in your dating and how you could make topics right.

Assuming you experience that you love your ex to an severe and need to relinquish every one of the unsightly reminiscences, then challenge out and inform your ex.

On the off danger that your ex likewise feels that they may address this dating, you'll probably have the choice to repair matters up in a rely of moments. Simply make sure that the harshness of the beyond isn't conveyed ahead on your ongoing dating.

On account of immoderate separations, it could require 5 to 10 months to get your ex over again. Be that as it is able to, a chance of constantly being not able to get them lower back assuming that your ex in no way in fact makes the relationship art work. In the event that your ex isn't always giving any indicators of improvement and your dating is once more at a junction, then it's far proper to surrender and hold on.

Chapter 3: Signs You Ought To Ponder

The number one aspect you can do is to try to take a gander at your situation unbiasedly and consider the ones items. You could alternatively not act excessively speedy and select to reunite spontaneously.

Trapped at the time

There are times even as you're crushed with such a whole lot of concern on the time which you pick out out to break up, without skipping a beat. It's tremendous not to allow yourself image to keep away from tracking down a goal.

Anything it is, your separation won't be very well examined and, after the air clears, you may discover yourself lamenting your preference.

If so, you need to chew the bullet, be humiliated, and request one greater opportunity. Best of suitable fortune

The circumstance

Perhaps you and your ex determined directly to go out in a top notch route since you each located your lives heading out in a one in all a kind course. Perhaps it changed into a far flung courting, and additionally you've got were given been no longer able to take the space.

Or however possibly taken into consideration genuinely one in all you is greater useless set on constructing a vocation than safeguarding the connection. Anything your justification inside the returned of your separation, it would were consistent at this point.

You also can have ended up in a superior spot in your existence now, and nearly approximately reuniting - which can honestly be what saves the connection the second time spherical.

What they said

Frequently, we're so trapped in our very non-public air pocket, we neglect about to test the hold near plan out. Generally, after a separation, cherished ones will suggest you to push aside your ex and preserve on.

They is probably correct. Regardless of whether you're grieved, they in all likelihood see aspects to your disintegrated romantic tale that your rose-shaded glasses could not see.

Yet, believe a state of affairs wherein they hold to will let you apprehend which you were moronic and insane and also you must get decrease lower back along side your ex. They may see that your relationship is definitely definitely nicely well worth saving, all subjects taken into consideration.

On the off danger which you attempt to see matters consistent with their angle, they might be accurate. At instances, your own family recognize you better than you realise your self, so listening to them one time only can also moreover moreover pay off.

Pitiably by myself

Have you at any thing prolonged beyond via a separation so terrible that someday later, you switch out to be hopeless to such an volume which you can not stand up, and you still count on most no longer possible, bleak contemplations?

Some say it is honestly a stage — that if you have hopeless sentiments and also you truely take shipping of you cannot live to tell the tale with out your ex it is a publish-separation display.

In any case, don't forget a situation wherein that level might now not disappear, and you are absolutely no longer the equal without your ex. Imagine a scenario wherein, after years have exceeded, you are as yet now not over *and also you be given you may in no way recover from* your ex.

The cherry on top here is that this: consider a scenario in which your ex feels the identical way. If so, then what is halting each of you? Simply reunite as of now!

Time

It's been said that point recuperates all injuries. Frequently, people without a doubt need time to anticipate, time to be without help from every body else, to be away, to boom, to recognize their missteps, and to widely recognized what they have got out of place.

You could have been childhood darlings who superior separation, but over the lengthy haul, you at ultimate did not bear in mind what forced you to break up, and all you keep in mind is the way in which they energized the ones butterflies to your stomach and the amount you absolutely love the man or woman.

After a while, the place became, the universe sincerely contrived to deliver you decrease again into every other's lives. Perhaps, previously, the timing have end up virtually off, and right now might be a extremely good possibility to begin over again. Stand with the useful resource of not to reunite.

Frequency

You like tom cats and he is hypersensitive to them. He adores Persian meals and also you cannot deal with the fragrance of flavors. You like matters coordinated and he's a lazy pig.

Incongruence is one of the vast drives that cut up up a couple. Imagine a situation wherein, after a while has elapsed, you've got a shift in angle and also you discover Persian cooking compelling.

In time, things will exchange and every of you can grow to be greater open to acclimating on your disparities. The scenario can be unique this time for each of you, and you can emerge as sharing all the extra nearly speaking, all things taken into consideration.

All subjects considered, you adjusted your perspective and desires after some time and had the choice to area topics proper right into a higher issue of view, making you a superior counterpart for each extraordinary.

Greener grass

Thus, the termination of your friendship has come, and you could not often maintain on to get yet again into dating any character another time.

Nonetheless, after one prearranged meet-up after an increasing number of a *and even though every other you would decide on neglect about*, you recognize that the grass truly isn't greener on the other thing.

As a remember of fact, beyond the wall is a stupid, spoiling no guy's land and also you'd prefer to move returned to in which you enjoy unique, thrilled, and alive.

This time, get higher over the wall, pass back in your grass, water it, hold it, and spot what's going to increase. So, assuming it's together with your ex that you'd definitely be completely happy and content material fabric, pull out all the stops!

ordel and wiser

At the aspect at the same time as we are greater younger, we will extra frequently than now not be juvenile and rash. Little topics frequently detonated into large battles. What's extra, how often did you take steps to cut up, up until you all at very last did?

Over the lengthy haul, you may think of yourselves as considering whether or no longer you need to were quite these days allow the ones reputedly insignificant statistics flow into, been instead extra expertise, and hung on.

It's completed. Yet, now which you're greater seasoned and smarter, you want to allow your ex any other possibility.

You experience positive that it's far going to be wonderful in moderate of the truth that you are each sufficiently mature to not misstep the identical way that brought on the realization of the friendship the preliminary time round.

Assuming that is you, permit that affection every different possibility.

Trusting in renewed opportunities

Assuming you are like a first-rate lot of the oldsters that during reality receive as true with in proper romance and sparkling possibilities, why now not permit your lost love some exceptional possibility?

There honestly isn't any written-in-stone desire which you can't reunite with an ex, so assuming it feels proper to you, why now not offer subjects one more possibility?

On the off risk which you realize that your ex dedicated an errors and you have have been given your very private weaknesses, as properly, then, at that factor, perhaps you're to be had to pardoning, neglecting, and pushing earlier.

In the event which you each although receive that you could decide out subjects, and will cope with having an effective dating, then move for it.

It modified into the brilliant of all time

There's now not some thing similar to actual affection. Whenever you have got had it, you recognise it!

You understand you determined "the satisfactory," and the equal goes in your ex. Notwithstanding, because of a few clarification, you had to head out in a distinctive route.

You attempted to move beyond that adoration you in truth take delivery of come to be the great love you'll at any factor have, yet completely not anything labored. You can't float beyond how astounding that individual is, and the manner in which you are wonderful for each different, irrespective of your singular flaws.

Chapter 4: Powerful Prayers To Get Your Ex Back

Nothing is more difficult and more painful than a separation. When our love leaves us, we sense that our lives are in risk and not anything could make us glad anymore. But we need to bear in mind that we've were given got the Almighty God. As lengthy as God is with us and we pray to Him, we need to by no means depression of carrying out some issue. So even to repair our love, we're capable of ask God to assist us restore our love and make our lives glad.

prayer to carry lower back out of place love

Loving Father, You are my savior and I apprehend that You pay attention this prayer and assist me get once more to my ex. Merciful God, bless me with Your religion and reputation and uplift me via Your unconditional love so I could make my ex come decrease again to me and love me all the time. Please deliver me information, O God, to comply with Your will. Great Lord, I don't have the coronary coronary heart to talk to him/her and ask him/her to miss approximately the past. Dear Lord, You are my protector and I be given as actual with Your terms once I recite a prayer to supply once more out of vicinity love. Listen to me, O God, and forgive me for disrespecting him/her. Mighty Lord in heaven, pay attention my requests because You are the quality person who can assist me for the duration of tough times. Amen.

Prayer for reconciliation with an ex

Loving Father, I typically call on you at some stage in difficult instances and I'm fantastic that you will pay attention to my prayer for reconciliation with my ex-accomplice. Gracious God, uplift me thru Your grace and bless me with Your recognition so I ought to make my ex-partner change his/her mind and are available again to me. Dear God, please pay attention to my coronary heart and assist me beautify my man or woman to the volume that I can impress him/her and growth the risk to rebuild our broken courting. Great Lord, You are my power and I recognize that You will assist me reconcile with my ex as quickly as viable. Great God in heaven, please pay interest my groaning as soon as I take a look at a prayer for my ex to come back once more lower back to me thinking about the truth that You are the first rate man or woman who can do wondrous topics. Amen.

Miracle prayer to get ex decrease returned

You are the Everlasting and Powerful Lord. You are my Merciful Lord. Holy Lord, thank You for imparting me with Your boundless blessings. Great Lord, I'm privy to my sins and, now, I repent for the times I ignored Your Will and chased idols. Dear Father, I'm definitely ashamed of my sins. My strength, please forgive me for now not putting Your Will in my coronary coronary coronary heart. Please forgive me, Holy Father, and function mercy on me. Gracious Lord, I Humbly ask You to be aware of me once I recite a miracle prayer to get my ex back because of the truth I want

Your help to do a little issue it takes to make my ex come back to me. Heavenly Father, supply me Your faith and permit Your phrases be normally on my thoughts and my lips once I take a look at a prayer for my ex to return lower decrease again to me. May Your glory help me pass forward, even in instances after I am doubtful and unsure. Amen.

Bible verses to get your ex lower once more

After the breakup, you shouldn't sense hopeless and depressed. Instead, you ought to located agree with inside the Merciful Lord's unconditional love and advantages and pray for rebuilding your damaged relationship as you test the following Bible verses to get your ex lower again. Don't forget about about that you want to be hopeful about getting lower decrease again collectively collectively with your ex due to the truth only the Almighty Lord is privy to the right time you could get again collectively.

Deuteronomy 7:9

"Know therefore that the LORD your God is God, the sincere God who maintains covenant and steadfast love with people who love him and keep his commandments, to a thousand generations."

Proverbs eight:17

"I love folks that love me, and people who are searching out for me diligently find out me."

Romans five:2-five

"Because of our faith, Christ has added us into this location of undeserved privilege wherein we now stand, and we with a piece of luck and joyfully appearance in advance to sharing God's glory. We could have a laugh, too, whilst we run into issues and trials, for we apprehend that they help us increase staying power. And staying energy develops power of person, and man or woman strengthens our assured need of salvation. And this desire will now not result in sadness. For we understand how absolutely God loves us because of the fact he has given us the Holy Spirit to fill our hearts with His love."

Psalm 86:15

"But you, O Lord, are a God merciful and gracious, sluggish to anger and abounding in steadfast love and faithfulness."

1 John 4: 18-19

"There isn't any fear in love. But best love drives out worry, due to the reality worry has to do with punishment. The person who fears isn't always made quality in love. We love every unique due to the fact he first cherished us."

Proverbs 10:12

"Hatred stirs up war, but love covers over all wrongs."

1 Corinthians thirteen:13

"And now the ones 3 stay: religion, wish and love. But the best of these is love."

Ephesians four:2

"Be actually humble and moderate; be affected person, bearing with every other in love."

Conclusion

God's advantages and select are subjects we want to exchange our lives. For this to seem we have to do topics that fulfill The Lord, and in go returned, He will provide us with His blessings. Every day, recite those varieties of prayers , and ask God to accept your request. Also, recite the prayer for a miracle proper now and make certain that Almighty God will make him/her come lower again to you.

Many clergies think the purpose that prayers can deliver achievement and prosperity is that they be a part of God's strength to us. On the alternative hand, scientists suppose it has inductive powers. Whatever the reason is, it's far apparent that prayers are effective. So I am glad this guide has provided sufficient prayers that will help you have a satisfying courting together along with your ex-lover.

Chapter 5: Battles Of Reuniting Together

Assuming you found reuniting together in conjunction with your ex is the amazing choice, keep in mind wherein you can pass from right right right here. Reuniting isn't always confident to mean cheerfully ever later, as there are, manifestly, many barriers you may must move.

This is particularly apparent in the event that your separation hasn't been so clean and there may be been a excellent deal of adverse phrases and mudslinging tossed the 2 one in all a kind tactics.

Here are the stuff you need to recall even as you are brooding about whether or not or now not reuniting can be the maximum best desire:

Hit rewind?

It's commonplace to overlook your ex and want to restore a past love hobby - however would it now not be truly helpful for you?

At the factor at the same time as you've got got been every contending and setting apart, there had been probable a extraordinary deal of warmed trades. There would possibly probably have moreover been excruciating, harsh phrases tossed round on the 2 factors.

In any case, with some work, genuineness, and pardoning on the 2 finishes, you may have the choice to preserve on even collectively.

Letting the cat out of the bag

Thus, subsequent to allow anyone understand the manner you detested your ex's guts and scorned essentially every little component approximately them... how are you going to visit permit the cat out of the bag which you've reunited

This can be quite abnormal, as you would possibly experience together with you owe a clarification to those nearest to you. Your smartest opportunity? Simply tell the reality.

Changing your mother and father' factor of view

There's moreover the hassle of attempting to modify your folks' perspectives in your ex.

At the issue even as you separated, you possibly decrease decrease lower back domestic to them crying and irate, letting them understand all of the "dreadful" things your ex did. Perhaps - probable - you helpfully overstated your story to color your then-accomplice in a terrible moderate.

So now which you're lower lower back together, how would likely you're making them like your ex another time? They'll probably advise you to definitely pass get every unique person.

Distance gambles

After all of the display and tears, there may be companions who will uphold your desire to reunite collectively together with your ex. Furthermore, there'll likewise be the folks who will possibly receive as real with you're insane.

You might also need to chance losing the trust of your partners, as they probably may not get in the back of your options in some time.

They need to likewise laugh at your hardships the subsequent time you approach them approximately troubles together with your ex, who is presently your companion all once more.

Virtual leisure whine

Obviously, there may be the difficulty of re-which consist of every different via on-line leisure all yet again. Furthermore, whilst you don't forget that no longer a few thing is mystery any similarly, humans will see this and begin speakme notwithstanding your well faith, as nicely.

On the off danger that that isn't always all, you can need to trade your courting fame all over again, and this will now not be not noted via partners who be careful for their notices.

Space for uncertainty

After all the problem and grief brought approximately thru your separation, your dating may not be the equal any further. You also can every inquiry your right idea techniques in compromise.

Research indicates that the those who professional separations and got lower returned with their ex have higher propensities closer to doubt. Tragically, that little bundle of uncertainty in the pit of your belly will constantly be there.

The preliminary now not many days or lengthy stretches of reuniting can also furthermore motive you to sense euphoric, however, you could have that voice closer to the rear of your head inquiring, "How prolonged is that this going to remaining this time?" Could you need to accompany a person who you do not really believe?

Is it some other courting

While it's miles not hard to select not to move on and let it torment you, reuniting implies that you every want to place forth a cognizant *and similarly hard* try and begin once more.

Does it resemble a few exceptional courting? You each want to type that one out. However, one factor is certainly: in the occasion that you stay as you've got been previously and do no longer roll out an improvement, then, at that component, your relationship is absolutely unwell-fated.

Chapter 6: Get Back With A Previous Sweetheart

Before we get right into a way to reunite with an ex, there are a couple of factors you should understand without skipping a beat.

Right off the bat, you can not direct mail their telephone, messages, Facebook, or a few particular form of online enjoyment with statements of remorse. That looks frantic and horrible and could not win them lower back. Regardless, an awesome manner to sincerely get your opportunities of returning your ex over again to nothing.

Furthermore, you cannot expect that they want to return slithering lower again with next to no paintings via any approach. Nor might you at any factor anticipate that they have got to want you lower again assuming you try to purpose your ex to sense green with envy by means of getting with every different character. This is the very last detail you recollect you must do to win once more your ex.

These are Gigantic no-nos if you have any preference to forever get your ex once more.

Anyway the connection finished, you have were given to tell the fact and forthright at the off chance that there may be to be a 2nd time round. Try now not to begin it on a misleading or mischievous premise.

Ensure that you spread the whole lot out on the desk and observe where it takes you. Perhaps the following time round can be manifestly superior to the primary.

Calling and messaging them continuously

You may also want to enjoy frantic to get your ex lower again, however you actually want to not act frantically. A frantic individual is a temper killer for the large majority. The justification behind an notable manner to be that it motives it to seem like you want self belief.

Individuals who love themselves are some distance greater stunning than dad and mom that do not. In this manner, don't call and text them continuously. Leave the ball in their courtroom.

Asking and trying to utilize sense sorry for

Similarly of calling and messaging continuously, you likewise don't have any preference to ask or request their pity. That is a casualty mind-set. You are presenting your ability to them.

Try not to do that. You really need to expose fearlessness. What's extra, whilst you ask your ex to reunite, you are not acting with self assurance. All subjects taken into consideration, have the demeanor of "everyone might also want me" no longer "no person goals me."

Allow them to trample you

In the event which you're seeing a topic right here, you are correct. On the off risk which you permit them to mistreat you or permit them to make the maximum of you, then you definitely do not regard your self.

Regardless of whether you do this, you need to surprise why you may want to reunite with an character who may do that to you. You must be with an man or woman who techniques you with deference.

Giving them fondness

This is like asking and arguing, no matter the fact that it appears to be particular. In the event which you are giving them a ton of friendship or gadgets, you're looking frantic yet again.

In this way, truly do no longer do that. That does now not endorse you can not be amicable and warm in a few cases, clearly do no longer allow it to transport too an extended manner into "franticness location".

Blowing a gasket at the same time as your ex beginnings relationship

Your ex may want to in all likelihood anyhow be single, however possibly they're not. All subjects considered, they're no longer in that frame of mind with you any in addition, in order that they will be currently persevering with on.

Assuming you determine out that they will be dating close to or seeing every other man or woman, do now not skip ballistic. It's no longer sudden and ordinary to do this after a separation, and they're authorized to appearance whomever they need.

Verbally abusing and outrage

In the occasion that you had a poisonous relationship or separation *or assuming which you are a dangerous man or woman*, do not depend on horrendous methods of behaving, for instance, ridiculing and outrage. This gets you simply no region.

In this manner, manage your feelings and sports activities. Nobody desires to reunite with any person who will mistreat them. All topics considered, you need to behave in addition to possible at the off threat which you're seeking to win them decrease lower back, accurate?

The fixation and mistakes

It's smooth for any person to be fixated on their ex to separate anyways. Be that as it may, fixation truely makes you appearance insane. Furthermore, no individual goals thus far an insane man or woman!

Additionally, heads up so that you do not misconstrue their phrases and sports activities sports. For instance, they may be performing well disposed inside the route of you, but that does not guarantee that they have got determined to reunite with you.

bankruptcy 7

HOW TO GET AN EX BACK AND GET THEM TO FORGIVE YOU

If you didn't do some thing unforgivable and also you realize how an entire lot you actually need to be with this individual, there are a few strategies you may use to get them again.

Just understand which you'll need to art work on it, and also you'll need to keep to artwork on being a better partner in case you do get your boyfriend or woman pal over again.

Do a few self - reflecting

We Don't Learn From Experience, We Learn From Reflecting On Experience

Without pondered image we skip blindly on our very very own way growing greater unintentional effects, and failing to achieve a few issue

Most human beings while we're accomplished with a courting we hardly ever make the effort to reflect on what turn out to be sincerely the hassle as in we genuinely reflect onconsideration on the fight not what brought about it and if we can we usually suppose the manner it grow to be our ex's fault however now not what really induced us or our ex's behavior or the relationship to cease.

The breakup reflected picture has elements; Self Reflection and Relationship Reflection wherein each has in reality three questions to ask yourself.

Self Reflection

1. What become my characteristic in completing the connection?; No keep in thoughts what the ex did, A courting is a way road. No more blame recreation, whilst we blame others for the whole thing we in no way trade because of the reality we don't see what's wrong with us. Our wrongdoings may be in subjects we name "not a massive deal" which may be a massive deal to our companions like now not giving quality time, dishonest (even the "it modified into only a kiss"), now not listening, anger problems and plenty of one-of-a-type subjects.

2. What will I do higher subsequent time?; This might not incredible be approximately changing what added on the split but additionally considering such things as in the next dating how are you going to be a higher companion, how can you take care of battle higher or how will you pick out a higher

companion or if you jumped on this courting too speedy then for the subsequent courting take your candy time and get to in reality recognize your functionality partner.

3. Should I be friends with my ex?; If you select to stay friends along side your ex, ask yourself why. I recommend , is it due to the fact they upload a few thing for your lifestyles like perhaps s/he's your commercial enterprise associate or coworker or is it out of false desire. If there's a kid worried you could need to discover a healthy manner of co-parenting together. Personally I assume it's dangerous to be buddies with an ex as it's smooth to get again with them despite the fact that we recognize it's now not going to workout session or get harm even extra as we see them pass on.

The Relationship Reflection

1. What went nicely?; No depend how awful the connection changed into or the accomplice modified into. There's constantly the tremendous in a few problem regardless

of how awful any scenario is. This will will permit you to realise what to preserve to the following dating.

2. What went incorrect?; I realise that could be a tough detail for folks who although love their exes and blame themselves for the finishing of the relationship. Here you in reality positioned on the black hat (horrible mind). If you simply answer this detail that is wherein maximum humans say "how should I be so dumb to position up with that" or "how can I probably deal with a person like that".

three. What did I examine?; So precisely what did you have a look at on this relationship. This may be top notch or awful, some element new you learnt within the dating or some factor one-of-a-type from past relationships in advance than that during case you had any.

Moving On...

If your trends had been the trouble within the beyond courting after a actual mirrored image you may realize a manner to be a higher accomplice to your next courting. If your associate grow to be the hassle, well you'll recognize what form of partner to pick to your next and with a piece of good fortune ultimate relationship.

You recognize the saying "A lesson is repeated until it's learnt" this truly applies within the good deal, even in relationships. If your associate have become the trouble and also you don't trade your type you'll come to be falling for the equal partner but with a terrific call and body. And if it have become you who changed into the trouble you will maintain on jumping from this relationship to each different or getting dumped till you discover ways to trade. These is probably the results we get due to the fact we don't studies and alternate.

If you're studying this and also you're unmarried, I want and want your subsequent relationship can be wholesome and gained't reason a cut up.

Think about it seriously

You want to consider whether or not or not this is a great idea or now not. Sure, you're emotional proper now, but you moreover may additionally moreover need to assume collectively along with your head.

How changed into the relationship? Were you without a doubt satisfied? More importantly, what made you cut up within the first area?

If it was a few factor extreme, like cheating, you then need to absolutely anticipate if that is the right man or woman for you.

Fix yourself up

Wipe away the ones tears and throw away the tissues. It's time to prevent crying and start being proactive about getting your ex back.

First of all, you need to seem like a person who is prepared to be in a dating all once more. Attraction is critical, and it all starts alongside aspect your appearance and way of life.

Be healthful, keep yourself in shape, and generally appearance your pleasant at the equal time as you go out. You in no manner understand at the same time as you may run into your ex, so it is able to help to hold your A-recreation 24/7.

We advocate it. The purpose of this is not to pander to your ex's appreciation for your appearance, but as an opportunity to beautify yourself-self assurance.

Show your self that you are worth of being loved, and your ex will soon see what they've been lacking out on.

If the breakup isn't ultra-modern, deliver your ex a text or a private message

Calling or just displaying up at your ex's region may be too ahead and too confrontational. It might probable make your ex definitely shielding, and they'll really shoot you down before you may even convey up the possibility of being together all over again.

Often, it's higher if you deliver a message alternatively, just to present your ex some time to reflect onconsideration on whether or not to answer or not.

If your ex replies amicably sufficient, then superb! If not, don't take it too for my part. Your ex is probably suspicious of your message.

Try to deliver some different message at another time, and preserve your palms crossed that you'll get a reaction.

If after approximately three messages, spanning over the route of constant with week or , you still get no response, there's a massive hazard that getting lower once more collectively is out of the question.

Admit your errors

You possibly don't want to understand what you've completed wrong, but if you want to be inside the function to get lower again with an ex or get them to at the least provide you with a threat, you need to very personal as a good buy as the wrong you've done.

You can't certainly count on your ex to take you decrease again if you overlook about the truth that you tousled. Admit your errors.

Tell your ex how wrong it become in case you need to perform a little aspect it's far you probably did to them. Make positive they realize that you understand the wrongdoing and you're aware of why it turned into tousled inside the first location.

Without doing so, don't expect that matters can be one of a type.

Even if you miraculously get lower again together without addressing the trouble, it'll come again to interrupt you up eventually. However, make sure that it's all actual and that you're no longer without a doubt pronouncing what you discovered they need to pay attention.

Also, please don't do it via text, as your ex may also probably absolutely assume you're no longer honest.

Give your ex an sincere apology

Sit them down and in reality make an apology to your ex proper now from the coronary coronary heart. If you truly need them yet again, then you definately truly are sorry.

If you're actually saying sorry for the sake of having again together and you don't genuinely advise it, they'll have the ability to tell. And they acquired't get once more with you.

Make super they recognize how sorry you actually are and that you understand how plenty some thing you probable did hurt them. Apologize, imply it, and apologize.

Elaborate

Explain your reasoning for why you want to get decrease decrease returned together. Make positive that they realize you're willing to change by manner of outlining your errors and telling them the way you're going to recovery subjects.

If you experience that your ex wishes to alternate as properly, this is the pleasant time to squeeze that during.

This is an all-or-not some thing verbal exchange, so it's incredible to get topics out of the manner early on. Do now not element hands as to who brought on the breakup.

Just tell your ex about the topics that you are willing to do to make topics higher.

Give them time to calm down

It's pretty everyday for human beings to need to get their ex lower back proper after breaking apart, however they'll in all likelihood be pretty disenchanted for a while if what you did have turn out to be awful enough to cause them to enjoy the want to go away you. That's top enough.

Contact your ex best to tell them how sorry you are, after which deliver them a few area. Don't bring up the difficulty of getting lower again collectively however, as your ex continues to be probably pissed currently.

They'll need to anticipate over what you've said without your have an impact on. And due to this they'll want to spend a while a ways from you.

Let your ex recognize which you'll supply them some time, after which don't touch them. It's adequate if your ex didn't reply.

Be affected individual and watch for them to move returned to you. Don't text your ex all of the time, even in case you anticipate that allows you to make you experience better. Doing this may only display your ex that you're decided.

Remember that it could take weeks or maybe months to get your ex returned. After all, they have got the proper to grieve after the breakup.

Keep calm while discussing the u . S . Of your dating

There's an splendid hazard which you'll get labored up and irritated if the opposite individual is asserting issues inside the relationship aside from what you probable did wrong. If you've damaged up, the possibilities are there are more troubles than really that one.

You want to stay calm while speaking to your ex. This individual is talking the problems so that you can art work to get beyond them.

They may also moreover moreover want to make your dating better and potentially get lower back collectively. Calm down and pay interest the entirety your ex has to mention.

Put yourself in their shoes

How have to you feel if they handled you the manner you've dealt with them? You'd probably be in reality damage and can've ended the relationship, too.

Put your self of their shoes and try to apprehend wherein they're coming from with everything. Gaining some mind-set will tremendous help your state of affairs.

Answer any questions they've got

They're entitled to invite a few questions even as you did some aspect to reduce to rubble that badly. Let them sit down down down and talk it with you. And solution their questions honestly and in reality.

Don't get disillusioned with a number of the questions they're asking, each. It's their right to impeach you at the same time as you've given them a lot heartache.

It's super to get yourself calm and solution what they ask you with the fact. You don't want to make the mistake of dropping your risk with the useful resource of

Make quality you're honestly listening

As your ex is speaking to you, make certain you're certainly paying attention to what they may be saying. It's smooth to location out or to virtually focus on what you need, however that is about them.

The high-quality manner to get your love lower decrease lower back is to pay attention their words, located yourself in their region, and examine their frame language.

Are they making eye contact and speaking to you in a smooth manner? Or are they maintaining off your eye and stumbling over their phrases?

If it's the latter, it could be that they're every shielding some element lower returned or feeling worried. By listening, you can workout what's taking location, and you can display them which you're in fact paying hobby.

Chapter 7: Why Do We Want To Recover What Has Been Lost?

Have you ever stopped to don't forget why some topics in lifestyles, as soon as we lose them, appear to tackle a terrific extra big fee than when they have been present? Maybe it's miles that antique, tired t-blouse we used to position at once to bed, or that memory of an antique childhood toy. However, nearly about relationships, specially love relationships, the importance of that feeling is infinitely greater profound.

Why is it that we are creatures who yearn so fervently for that this is lengthy long long past?

As we begin this introspection, it's far critical to understand that the desire to regain what has been out of place isn't absolutely a superficial whim or impulsive response. In many times, this sense is rooted deep interior our psychology and our essence as people. We are, anyways, beings of connections, and it's far natural that after this type of connections is broken or fades away, we sense an emptiness.

The loss of a courting, in particular, regularly leaves an indelible mark on our lives. The feelings that are aroused, on the aspect of remorse, longing and from time to time even remorse, are immoderate and may be overwhelming. But what if I knowledgeable you that there can be a deeper motive in the back of all of it, a reason this is going beyond actually looking to get yet again together with that character? What if I cautioned you that information that motive can be the vital component to not best getting your ex lower again, but additionally to coming across your self in a manner you in no way imagined?

The British logician Alan Watts, in his paintings "The Book of Taboo" (1966), proposes a charming idea: lifestyles, in essence, is a exercise of cover-and-are attempting to find that we play with ourselves. We look for some element that, in truth, we've got never out of region. This attitude, although it appears to consult spirituality and the look for due to this, moreover may be carried out to our relationships. In losing a person, we won't first-class be mourning the loss of that unique man or woman, however moreover the shortage of a part of ourselves, a reflected picture of our identification that became contemplated in that dating.

So what clearly drives us to need that person decrease returned? Is it actually love and companionship that we pass over, or is there something deeper, some element intrinsically related to our search for identity and purpose?

These are not really rhetorical questions to make you scratch your head. Rather, they may be invitations that allows you to dive into deep reflection and recognize the "why" at the back of your emotions and moves. Because, don't forget me, this "why" might be your compass on this adventure, guiding you inside the route of right reconciliation, not nice with that particular person, but with yourself.

So, costly reader, as you embark on this introspection, I inspire you to carry out that with sincerity, courage and, in particular, an open thoughts. The method to the query "Why will we need to reclaim what was misplaced?" can also additionally surprise, venture and in the long run free up you. And preserve in mind, this is genuinely the start. There is a big international of discovery watching for you within the coming chapters. For now, take a deep breath, concentrate for your coronary heart and put together to embark on one of the maximum transformative trips of your existence.

By the manner, if you ever marvel approximately the mental basis of breakups, don't worry. We'll delve greater into that during Chapter 2. But first, allow's maintain this introspection. After all, each extremely good adventure begins offevolved offevolved with a unmarried step, or in this case, a unmarried query.

Now, as we discover extra deeply the selection to reclaim what we've out of region, we are capable of approach a substantial sort of theories and perspectives that offer us lighting fixtures in this direction. Esther Perel's artwork, "The State of Unions" (2017), for example, shows that current relationships are enormously specifically charged. Today, we assume our accomplice to be a lover, a chum, a financial associate, a co-determine, and lots more. When we lose that man or woman, we are not just losing a love, but a complex internet of connections and roles they completed in our lives.

Psychologist Harriet Lerner in "Dance of Anger" (1985) explores how relationships frequently falter no longer due to the fact love is missing, however due to the fact humans do now not have the gadget to talk and recognize each first-rate in instances of strain or battle. The loss of a relationship also can, in fact, be the symptom of a deeper trouble, related to our private insecurities, fears, and lack of communique skills. In asking ourselves why we need to regain what we've out of place, we can be, deep down, searching out a 2d chance to accurate mistakes, to examine and to expand.

On a few other angle, have you ever ever ever considered that the act of reclaiming is probably greater than truely rekindling a beyond relationship? It can be an possibility to recover a out of place a part of oneself. Carl Jung, the renowned psychoanalyst, talked considerably about the concept of the "self" in his writings, especially in "The Self and the Unconscious" (1928). He recommended that during our lives, we bypass some distance from this right "self" because of various outside pressures and existence studies. Could it is that, in looking for to get our ex-partner decrease lower back, we also are searching for to get in the direction of that actual "self"? Perhaps, in that person, we located a mirrored image of who we were, or who we aspired to be.

These perspectives, though seemingly divergent, converge on a vital point: the selection to get higher what become out of place isn't always a superficial journey. It is a deep adventure interior, a look for statistics, growth and, in the end, recuperation.

But what if I knowledgeable you which you aren't on my own on this journey? In reality, there are countless human beings who have walked this route before you, and characteristic left at the back of treasured instructions and tools. So, as you still navigate this bankruptcy, I invite you to open your mind and coronary heart to those views. Allow those thoughts to assignment you, inspire you and, most significantly, guide you.

Don't neglect about, high priced reader, that each step you take on this journey, each net web page you turn and every reflected picture you're making, brings you one step in the course of that final reason. Whether that purpose is reconciliation collectively together with your ex or without a doubt a reconciliation with your self, the journey, with all its americaand downs, might be properly really worth it.

Let's take a journey again in time, a piece concept check. Imagine you are in a library. This library is particular as it includes all the memories, moments and emotions of your beyond relationship. Now, select a ebook from those cabinets, any ebook that represents a specially robust reminiscence with that man or woman. Open its pages and relive that 2d. What do you spot? What do you experience? What phrases, smells and sounds come for your mind?

This exercising may seem easy, however it has a selected purpose: to spotlight the intensity and richness of the human reviews anyone share. Every courting, each 2nd, leaves an indelible mark at the canvas of our life. As Brené Brown factors out in her artwork "The Power of Vulnerability" (2012), we're glaringly related beings, and people connections, whether or not or no longer great or painful, define who we are.

Inside that imaginary library, there are possibly books of happy moments, unhappy moments, and moments you can alternatively forget. But, and this is the vital factor, all of these moments are part of your history. And while you extended to get higher what you have got out of region, in lots of techniques, you're longing to relive and rewrite a number of the ones chapters.

Let me percentage an example that would shed some slight on this idea. Alicia and Roberto have been a pair for five years. During that component, they shared laughter, tears, journey and moments that neither of them might ever neglect approximately about. However, as regularly takes location, matters frayed, priorities changed and sooner or later they separated. Years later, Alicia determined herself visiting the city wherein they met, and each corner, each café, every alley reminded her of Roberto. Not that she continually wanted to transport lower lower back to him, however she longed for the revel in of belonging, connection and adventure they as quickly as shared.

What Alicia did now not apprehend have emerge as that, notwithstanding the truth that Roberto became part of the ones recollections, what she in fact longed for changed into part of herself that she felt she had lost within the procedure. At its center, she desired to recapture that experience of adventure, ardour and interest that had characterized that degree of her life.

Perhaps, like Alice, what you honestly lengthy for is not definitely the individual, however what that man or woman represented on your lifestyles. As Viktor Frankl stated in "Man's Search for Meaning" (1946), it's far the that means in our lives that offers us cause. And occasionally, it is through relationships that we discover that that means.

Now, does this mean that you ought to abandon all attempts at reconciliation? Certainly now not. However, through records the depths of your desire, you can method any strive at recovery with renewed readability and, likely, with more large reason.

After all, at the same time as we attempt to regain what we've got had been given misplaced, we're frequently seeking out something a good buy large and deeper than truly reliving vintage recollections. We are looking for know-how, redemption and, in the long run, non-public increase. You are within the device of unraveling the ones layers, and each layer you discover brings you one step toward the fact you're attempting to find.

Now, with a clearer statistics of the severa sides and depths of the desire to get better what we've out of place, a crucial question arises: What can we do with this statistics? This solution, steeply-priced reader, has as many dimensions because of the fact the motivations which have introduced us thus far. But, in essence, it boils all the way right down to a single phrase: movement.

It is easy to get caught inside the cycle of introspection and mirrored photograph. While treasured, there comes a time when we need to use what we have got found out and observe it in the actual global. As Rollo May states in "The Courage to Create" (1975), the real motive of perception is not virtually to understand, however to act on that understanding.

So how can we observe this epiphany? First, via spotting that, on the same time as getting again an ex-partner may be a intention, reconciliation with oneself is further, if no longer extra, critical. Every relationship, even people who've ended, gives us a very specific opportunity to analyze, expand and evolve as human beings.

Next, it's far essential to recollect that at the identical time as the training of the beyond are critical, the prevailing is wherein the real magic occurs. Here and now could be in that you have were given the power to make selections, trade styles and, in case you need, try reconciliation.

And speakme of reconciliation, John Gottman, in "The Seven Principles for Making Marriage Work" (1999), gives us with a vital notion: reconciliation is not actually about reliving the beyond, but approximately building a modern-day future. So, as you contemplate getting again together at the side of your ex, keep in mind not most effective what turned into, but what is going to be.

Finally, as with each journey, it is critical to have an outstanding time the small accomplishments along the way. Whether it's far a lifestyles-converting insight or certainly an afternoon in which you revel in more at peace at the side of your beyond, each jump forward merits to be recognized.

In recapping, we've got navigated collectively through the complexities of human preference, the yearning for connection and the search for which means. We have explored expert views, actual-life examples and, most importantly, we have got launched into a adventure inside the path of self-knowledge.

I desire that, armed with this statistics, you revel in empowered to face the subsequent bankruptcy of your life, something it could be. And if you're wondering what is next, well, the solution awaits you in the subsequent chapters. Next, we are able to delve into the depths of the psychology in the again of breakups and find out how know-how grief can be the important trouble to overcoming it. I promise, it's miles going to be an eye fixed fixed fixed-beginning journey. Until then, live curious, courageous and normally willing to investigate.

Chapter 8: The Psychology Behind Breakups

Have you ever felt that knot in your belly that unbearable emptiness, on the identical time as confronted with the fact of a breakup? As if the world as you knew it had modified and also you placed yourself in an unknown terrain, plagued via uncertainty and ache. However, that lets in you to go with the flow ahead, to get better, and even to shut chapters, it's miles important to understand the psychology within the returned of this ache and breakups. Why? Because thru the usage of know-how the character of grief, we're capable of find greater powerful equipment to address it, conquer it and finally use it for our personal boom.

The ache of a breakup isn't clearly emotional. In reality, modern-day studies have tested that the thoughts techniques the emotional ache of a breakup similarly to physical ache. Surprised? You're now not on my own on this. Science has over and over tested us that our brains do now not efficiently differentiate amongst physical and emotional pain. So on the same time as we say that a breakup "hurts," it isn't always handiest a metaphor.

But, past the natural response, there's the complicated tangle of emotions and recollections that accompany a dating. Every shared chortle, each communicate, each intimate second weaves together to shape a tale that, as soon as interrupted, leaves a void in our private facts. And that is where psychology performs a important function.

Have you ever stopped to bear in mind at what unique 2d you felt that wrenching pain? Was it proper after the breakup? Or have become it afterwards, at the same time as you came inside the route of a reminiscence, a photograph, or a clean melody that evoked you? The manner of coping with a breakup is deeply personal and but as an opportunity regular.

Throughout this financial catastrophe, I will manual you thru the tough psychology within the back of breakups. We will clear up collectively the threads of feelings, reflect on how our minds method ache and, most importantly, discover how we are able to use this realize-the way to heal and develop.

Before continuing, I invite you to invite yourself a question: What do you want to benefit with the resource of statistics the ache of your breakup? Is it certainly to alleviate your struggling? Or is there a deeper quest, a quest for records, boom and in all likelihood redemption?

This introspection is vital due to the fact, as within the previous bankruptcy, the "why" will guide your course. I inspire you to dive into this journey with an open mind and a willing coronary heart. Because, on the give up of the day, it's far not quite lots facts ache, however about how we cope with it, conquer it and redecorate it into a stress for proper in our lives.

Diving deeper into this ocean of feelings, it is crucial to endure in mind the psychology in the back of how we revel in and way grief.

According to Elisabeth Kübler-Ross, in her influential artwork "On Death and Dying" (1969), humans undergo five levels of grief: denial, anger, bargaining, melancholy, and reputation. Although first of all performed to grieving over loss of life, those ranges are rather applicable to like breakups. We face the lack of a relationship as though we're mourning some thing valuable that has handed away.

Think approximately it. At first, denial protects us from the preliminary wonder, allowing us to take time to manner what is taking place. How usually have you informed yourself that "it can not be right" or that "the next day the whole lot is probably decrease lower returned to everyday"? But, ultimately, reality units in, and anger emerges. It can be in opposition in your ex-associate, in the direction of your self, or perhaps in competition to outdoor factors.

However, this anger isn't simply a bad feeling. As Dr. Steven Stosny stated in "Love Without

Wounds" (2008), anger is mostly a protection mechanism, an try to guard our wounded vanity. Therefore, it is essential to apprehend it, receive it, and way it constructively.

Negotiation is the following phase, and this is often wherein many get stuck. "If best I had performed this" or "if fine I had said that," are not unusual manifestations of this level. It is a decided attempt to regain manage, to agree with that we ought to have finished some thing one in each of a kind to trade the outcome.

Depression, in spite of the truth that painful, is a sign that we are beginning to truly accept reality. It is a herbal reaction to loss and is often positioned through using attractiveness, wherein we begin to find out peace with the situation.

These levels aren't linear. You can circulate from one to every other in any order, and you could cross again to earlier stages. But, by using the use of being aware about those levels and what they suggest, you're armed with the understand-the manner to navigate them effectively.

In addition to know-how those levels, it's far vital to apprehend how our personal private histories and beyond traumas can have an impact on our revel in of a breakup. Each oldsters brings to the connection baggage, product of beyond reviews, hurts and fears. When going via a breakup, those wounds can resurface, intensifying the ache and complicating the restoration device. Dr. Sue Johnson in "Created for Love" (2011) stresses the importance of spotting and addressing those underlying wounds so that you can heal holistically.

But what if I advised you that there are methods to transform this ache, to apply it as a catalyst for profound private growth? That is precisely the jewel located in adversity, and inside the following sections, we're able to remedy a manner to do in reality that.

Let me percentage the tale of Laura, a close pal who went through a disturbing breakup along facet her accomplice of seven years, Miguel. From the outside, they seemed like the right couple. They shared dreams, travels and huge love. However, whilst the connection ended, Laura located herself in a pit of despair. In the primary few weeks, she couldn't break out from bed, the load of grief anchoring her. But eventually, she decided that in choice to sinking into sadness, she may channel her pain into some factor tremendous.

Laura started out attending writing workshops. At first, her terms were truely an extension of her ache, however through the years, she placed in writing a manner to approach her emotions. With each written word, she felt a touch lighter. A three hundred and sixty five days later, Laura published a ebook of poetry about love, loss and recovery, turning her private enjoy proper into a source of concept for others.

Laura's story isn't always particular. Throughout records, many have used art work, song and literature as tactics to technique and conquer grief. In "The Lament for Icarus" (1938), British poet W. H. Auden speaks of transformation via artwork, suggesting that paintings gives us with a manner to confront and unique our non-public feelings.

But you don't want to be an artist to transform grief. Sometimes, it may be as smooth as beginning a cutting-edge hobby, joining a useful resource agency, or truly taking a step back and reevaluating your priorities and dreams. The essential concept is to discover a optimistic outlet to your feelings, in choice to allowing them to consume you.

Sometimes the pain of a breakup can deliver unresolved problems from our past to the floor. For David, every different friend, his breakup with Clara changed into devastating now not simplest due to the lack of the relationship, however because it reminded him of his painful relationship together with his absent father. It modified into best at the same time as he confronted those underlying emotions and sought remedy that he come to be capable of begin the real healing technique.

Herein lies every other crucial lesson. Our past traumas, hurts and fears do not disappear genuinely due to the truth we neglect approximately them. Instead, they lie dormant, affecting our alternatives and reactions. It is handiest via handling the ones inner demons that we're capable of truely free ourselves from their have an effect on.

I want that through sharing the ones reminiscences, you recognize which you aren't on my own in this adventure. We all, in a few unspecified time inside the destiny in our lives, face the pain of loss. However, with the proper device and a increase-orientated mind-set, that ache can be the catalyst for deep and giant transformation.

Human nature is, via way of default, resilient. Even in our darkest hours, we've have been given an innate potential to find mild, to search for meaning and reason, and to rebuild ourselves from the wreckage. Psychologist Carol Dweck, in her e-book "Growth Mindset: The New Psychology of Success" (2006), posits that our attitude inside the face of disturbing conditions, failures and adversity can dictate the route of our healing. Those with a increase thoughts-set see limitations as opportunities to take a look at and increase. This mindset, at the same time as clean, is exceedingly effective.

Now, you will be wondering, "That sounds splendid in idea, but how does it workout in reality?" Well, this is in which actual introspection is to be had in. It is in spotting our feelings, facts their foundation and confronting them face to face, in which we find right freedom. As the fact seeker Friedrich Nietzsche noted, "He who has a why to stay for, can endure nearly any how."

So what is your "why" - why do you select out to face this pain, understand it, and with a piece of achievement triumph over it? The solutions are as numerous due to the fact the human beings, however at their middle, we all are looking for the equal element: peace, knowledge and a revel in of motive.

Reviewing what we have got got included to date, we can see that the psychology within the decrease lower back of breakups is not actually a topic of textbooks and theories. It is deeply human, steeped in emotions, traumas and dreams. It is a journey that takes us from the depths of despair to the heights of information.

So, as we circulate in advance in this journey, I invite you to stay open, reflective and, distinctly, type to your self. Recovery is not a linear way, however with the right guidance and a resilient spirit, it's far truly potential.

The subsequent monetary spoil will lead us to find out romantic love and the manner our expectations, often inspired with the useful resource of society and way of life, may not be as sensible as we belief. An charming journey awaits you, entire of revelations and discoveries. Together, we're able to demystify romantic love and discover ways to gather relationships primarily based totally on authenticity and expertise. Until then, I go away you with one concept: actual boom regularly starts offevolved in which our consolation region ends. Are you geared up to take the jump?

Chapter 9: Demystifying Romantic Love

Have you ever felt that love, as portrayed in well-known films, collection and songs, looks as if an improbable best? If so, you are no longer on my own. Romantic love has been, for loads of years, portrayed as a rapturous feeling that, as soon as determined, solves all our troubles and leads us to stay "fortuitously ever after." But what occurs even as these excellent clashes with truth?

What if I knowledgeable you that a whole lot of what you take delivery of as genuine with approximately romantic love is primarily based totally totally on myths and cultural expectations that, in vicinity of supporting us, regularly avoid us in our quest for wholesome and pleasurable relationships? Are you inclined to impeach what you've got taken as a proper till now?

In this bankruptcy, we're able to take a deep test romantic love, distilling truth from fantasy and supplying you with machine to assemble a courting based totally totally on mutual understanding, authenticity and recognize. But in advance than we dive into it, it's miles essential that you ask your self: why is this mission rely essential to you? Are you looking for a courting based mostly on truths or would probable you as an alternative be given illusions?

The global of romantic love, as we recognise it, is rife with expectancies. From a younger age, we're taught to expect that our "higher half of of" will complete us, that real love overcomes any impediment, and that if some thing does not work out, it is because perhaps it wasn't "actual love." But these ideas, while comforting, can result in horrific dating styles and the perpetuation of beliefs that do not serve us in actual life.

Renowned psychologist Erich Fromm, in his e-book "The Art of Loving" (1956), argues that love isn't always surely a passive sensation, however an artwork that requires understanding and attempt. He argues that our cutting-edge way of life sees love generally as an revel in that "falls" in choice to a capabilities that is evolved and nurtured.

And therein lies the problem. We had been conditioned to simply accept as genuine with that love is something that truly "takes place," at the same time as not having to paintings at it. However, any a fulfillment, lengthy-term relationship will allow you to recognize that love takes art work, conversation and, in reality, self-attention.

It's time to position fairy tales apart and look at love from a more mature and practical angle. Throughout this bankruptcy, I will guide you through this approach of discovery and, collectively, we're capable of redefine what love technique within the real global. Are you organized to embark in this journey?

As we demystify romantic love, it is crucial to recognize that lots of our ingrained ideals originate in testimonies and traditions that have been surpassed down through generations. These narratives, even as poetic and charming, regularly set unrealistic necessities for what a courting need to be.

Take, for example, the concept that genuine love by no means dies. This romantic perception has been popularized in infinite films, novels and ballads. However, as sociologist Anthony Giddens elements out in "The Transformation of Intimacy" (1992), relationships within the modern-day technology are greater fluid and less described via conventional norms. People now are attempting to find authenticity, emotional connection and equality of their relationships, in place of mere permanence.

Another not unusual fantasy is the concept that our perfect companion "completes" us. This notion, regularly popularized within the media, insinuates that we're incomplete beings seeking out every other individual to make us entire. Bell hooks, in "All About Love: New Visions" (2000), argues that this form of mentality can bring about codependent and toxic relationships. Instead of searching out a person to "complete" us, we need to attempt to be entire, self-sufficient those who select to share their lives with others.

Moreover, love is not commonly serene and non violent. We are regularly suggested that if we like someone, the whole thing is probably easy and without conflict. However, this can not be similarly from the reality. Psychologist Harriet Lerner, in "Dance of Anger" (1985), shows that conflict, while approached in a wholesome manner, can be a device for increase and facts in relationships.

It is important that we flow into away from these idealized notions and begin to view love and relationships from a extra sensible and stage-headed perspective. In doing so, we no longer fine loose ourselves from unrealistic expectancies, however also open the door to more actual, great and fantastic relationships.

But how do we achieve this factor of reputation and understanding? How can we set aside the memories we were listening to all our lives and start to write down down our non-public? Let us maintain in this journey of demystification and discovery, and discover together the real artwork of loving in the present day-day worldwide.

Let's use a realistic example to demonstrate this. Imagine a couple: Sara and Alejandro. From a younger age, every have been fed stories of love that promise everlasting, unbroken happiness. Now, years into their dating, they discover themselves in a disaster. Alejandro believes that if he feels any doubt or dissatisfaction, possibly he is not in the proper relationship. After all, shouldn't the whole thing be first rate within the event that they without a doubt love each exclusive? On the other hand, Sara feels she need to disguise her insecurities and fears, as showing vulnerability ought to push Alejandro away. But is that this the truth of affection?

Drawing thought from Isabel Menéndez's "The Myths of Romantic Love" (1998), we will see that those worries are born of unrealistic expectations. Love is, in essence, a constant dance among closeness and autonomy, ardour and everyday, giving and receiving. It is, with the resource of nature, imperfect and evolving.

Another instance to recall is the popularized belief of "love inside the beginning sight". It's a idea that has been extolled in infinite literary works and films. But how many prolonged-lasting, healthful relationships do you apprehend of that certainly started that manner? Daniel Jones, editor of the New York Times' "Modern Love" column, has said on numerous events that the most poignant and actual stories are not the ones of chance encounters that motive immediate love, however individuals who chronicle the challenges, compromises and boom of couples through the years.

So, if you locate yourself questioning your very non-public relationships primarily based on the ones narratives, it's time to pause and reflect. Are you chasing a pipe dream or are you willing to embark at the hard but worthwhile adventure of building actual love?

After all, love isn't always a vacation spot, but a adventure. And like all journey, it's going to consist of its united statesand downs. The key is knowing a manner to navigate through them, armed with records, staying power and, most importantly, authenticity. It is time to observe love not as an no longer viable ideal, however as a continuously evolving human enjoy.

But what takes region at the same time as we set aside the fairy testimonies and take a look at love through a clearer, greater practical lens? We discover that, some distance from being a linear narrative with a assured satisfied finishing, love is a complex internet of feelings, alternatives and compromises.

Erich Fromm, in "The Art of Loving" (1956), argues that to absolutely love is an art, a knowledge that must be found and practiced. It is not in fact a experience that arises spontaneously, but a conscious choice we make each day. And, as with every artwork, it calls for determination, staying strength and, every so often, the willingness to start over.

Now wherein does this go away us - does it advocate we should discard all of the romantic memories and films we have fed on over time? Not always. Instead, we are able to use them as tools to mirror on our non-public beliefs and expectancies. By recognizing the myths of romantic love, we're better organized to chart our personal direction, one which resonates with our truth and experience.

It is critical that we arm ourselves with this knowledge and mind-set. As we flow into ahead in our look for love and connection, having a strong know-how of what's actual and what's idealization will function a useful compass.

As we end this financial ruin, I invite you to introspect. Think about your non-public relationships and beliefs about love. What narratives have you ever allowed to manual your moves and selections? As you keep reading, I will provide you gear and insights that will help you cultivate a greater genuine and extensive love.

Don't allow myths hold you once more. In the following economic disaster, we can deal with the significance of personal rebuilding and the way you can start to construct a robust basis for yourself, no matter your relational reputation Because, on the quit of the day, the adventure to right love starts offevolved offevolved with yourself. Go earlier, there is loads greater to discover and research.

Chapter 10: Personal Reconstruction

It is charming how the most solid and resilient systems are often erected on the foundations of a few factor that has collapsed. But why is that this applicable with regards to the landscape of our emotional being?

Have you ever stopped to bear in thoughts that, frequently, right self-introduction starts offevolved offevolved after a deconstruction? Perhaps, after a dating that has fallen apart or a dream that has did now not materialize. At the prevent of the day, the most tough opinions frequently turn out to be the maximum formative.

Let me ask you a question, pricey reader: Have you ever felt that, after a particularly tumultuous period for your life, you emerged with a clearer, extra subtle version of your self? If your answer is sure, you are not by myself. And if no, you're on the right route to that discovery.

Understanding the significance of personal reconstruction is vital for any person seeking out to increase, evolve and, positive, in all likelihood move again to an antique love with a renewed thoughts-set. But before we dive into the depths of a way to do this, it's miles vital to apprehend why it is so important.

When considering physical systems, houses, for instance, one might probably argue that their strength lies in their foundations. But, sarcastically, the actual test in their patience is not how well they hold up at some stage in proper times, however how they maintain up within the route of storms.

Human beings are similar. On the floor, absolutely everyone positioned on masks, roles and personalities that we show to the world. But whilst these outer layers are stripped away, whether or not or now not through ache, loss or adversity, we find our truest essence. In that vicinity of vulnerability and self-discovery, lies the possibility to rebuild.

Carl Rogers, a mentioned psychologist and one of the predominant exponents of customer-targeted remedy, argued in his paintings "The Process of Becoming a Person" (1961) that we're all on a adventure toward self-focus. He counseled that each person has inherent potential that may be cultivated and superior through knowledge and splendor.

If that is right, and I firmly do not forget it's miles, then any scenario that leads us to confront and study our most real self is a blessing in conceal. Yes, even breakups. Especially breakups.

Before you delve any similarly into this concept, I invite you to take a deep breath and open your thoughts and coronary coronary heart to the opportunity that the "prevent" you've got got experienced may additionally moreover in truth be the begin of some element wonderfully new and transformative.

Now, with that data, let's bypass on to the mechanics and strategies of private reconstruction. I promise you, the adventure is properly honestly well worth it.

In Leonardo da Vinci's time, towns devastated by way of way of time or battle had been often rebuilt on their very private ruins. These reconstructions had been not seen truly as renovation, however alternatively as a alternate, an possibility to innovate and reinvent. Following this analogy, consider your private emotional or intellectual "ruins." They are not a reminder of what you've got were given misplaced, but a canvas upon which you could sculpt your subsequent masterpiece.

Think of James, as an instance. After his separation with Martha, his relationship of 5 years, he felt out of vicinity. Life, as he knew it, had been uprooted. But what if I instructed you that James located his real ardour at some point of this period of desolation? He immersed himself in writing, and in plenty less than a yr, he had now not only recovered emotionally, but had published his first e-book of poetry. The loss was his catalyst.

Or keep in mind Elaina, who after being laid off from her lifelong job, determined to travel the arena. During her travels, she positioned her love for photos and commenced documenting her evaluations. Today, her photographs decorate the walls of galleries and houses alike.

What do James and Elaina have in commonplace? They both faced adversity, positive, however similarly they positioned an opportunity to rebuild in the midst of chaos.

So how can you embark on your non-public private rebuilding journey? Here are a few examples and tips, based on research and writings from specialists inside the situation:

1. Self-reflected picture: In "Man's Search for Meaning" (1946), Viktor Frankl argues that between stimulus and reaction, there's a vicinity. In that area, we've the power to pick our response. And in that preference, lies our freedom and increase. So take a 2nd to mirror. What has added you this a long

manner? What have you discovered? Where do you need to go?

2. Skill development: As Robert Greene shows in "Mastery" (2012), mastery of any skills is a way that would take an entire existence. But in that journey, we find out no longer exceptional the capacity itself, however moreover hidden factors of ourselves. Learning some thing new, whether or not or not or no longer it's miles a language, a musical device, or every other functionality, may be pretty healing and enriching.

three. Connection: As Brené Brown mentions in "The Power of Vulnerability" (2012), vulnerability is the cradle of innovation and exchange. Connecting with others, sharing your reviews and being attentive to theirs can provide you with a today's perspective and assist you on your path to rebuilding.

These are virtually beginning factors. Your adventure may be unique, advocated thru your opinions, your dreams and your goals.

But don't forget, the act of rebuilding does no longer mean forgetting or replacing what has been misplaced. It way honoring the ones experiences and using them as a basis to bring together some thing even extra. Are you prepared to embark in this interesting adventure?

The act of rebuilding, in essence, is a assertion of resistance and resilience. Like a tree that has been battered via a storm, but remains firmly rooted to the ground, geared up to flourish yet again, you could moreover find out electricity on your very personal roots and grow once more.

Ask yourself this question: What detail of yourself, which you can have left out or not explored in advance than, can be the important thing for your rebirth? Stephen Covey, in "The 7 Habits of Highly Effective People" (1989), highlights the significance of "sharpening the observed," regarding the consistent want to renew and reinvent ourselves. It isn't always a one-time system, but a non-stop exercise of self-evaluation and growth.

Some discover solace and clarity in art work. Consider Gabriela's tale. After her breakup, she started out painting, permitting her emotions to translate into vibrant canvases whole of coloration and motion. Through the technique, she no longer simplest positioned a passion, however additionally a way to machine her feelings and discover peace. As Julia Cameron proposes in "The Artist's Way" (1992), creativity can be a powerful device for self-discovery.

Others, like Daniel, discover clarity in physical motion. After going via a series of limitations in his life, he decided to look at yoga. What started out out as an occasional exercising became a profound journey of self-discovery and recuperation. As Daniel immersed himself within the postures, he began to launch emotional and intellectual tensions. B.K.S. Iyengar, in "Light on Yoga" (1966), describes yoga now not best as a physical practice, however as a adventure into oneself, a deep introspection that allows for reconnection and rebalancing.

But past person memories and the high-quality paths one may also absorb their reconstruction, there can be a commonplace thread: the innate desire to go past situations and find out deeper motive and which means that.

To end this chapter, I would love you to reflect at the terms of Carl Rogers, one of the maximum influential psychologists of the 20th century, who in "The Process of Becoming a Person" (1961), emphasizes that everybody very very own an internal ability for growth and self-attention. The secret's to pay attention to that inner voice, that whisper that courses us in the route of our first rate version.

Now, as you put together for the subsequent financial damage, reflect onconsideration on this: What gear and practices will help you communicate better with the ones spherical you? Because, as you'll discover, powerful communication is an important piece within the puzzle of self-discovery and rebuilding. See you inside the subsequent economic smash, in which we're going to find out the artwork and technological expertise at the back of right conversation.

Chapter 11: Communication And Its Secrets And Techniques And Strategies

In the eternal dance of human relationships, there may be no device extra powerful and but greater misunderstood than communique. Have you ever at a loss for words why, irrespective of talking the equal language as each other man or woman, you once in a while seem to come back back from absolutely one-of-a-type worlds? You aren't by myself. But proper right here lies a important query: How can communication, that maximum fundamental of tools, be every our greatest strength and our nice weak spot?

Communication is the glue that holds societies, households and, positive, couples together. But have you ever ever stopped to reflect onconsideration on what it truely manner to speak? We're not surely speakme about terms, but gestures, tones of voice, pauses, appears. These are all processes of speaking. And, often, it's miles what we don't say in words that screams the loudest.

In a relationship, whether or not or now not romantic, familial or friendly, understanding and being understood is the vital factor to installing region deep and terrific connections. But why, if communique is so vital, are we able to frequently locate ourselves suffering with it? The answer can be deeper than you observed.

As you dive into this bankruptcy, I assignment you to consider conversation from a broader thoughts-set. Why do you find out that, even even as you assume you are being smooth, the man or woman you're speakme to does not understand you? Or why, in moments of hysteria, phrases seem to fail?

Before we dive into the depths of the art work and technological knowledge of verbal exchange, I'd together with you to mirror on one idea: active listening. Active listening goes past truly being attentive to what someone is saying; it is about being gift, paying whole interest, decoding and information the message in its entirety. If you have got got ever felt that someone have become now not "in reality listening" to you, you were likely perceiving a loss of lively listening.

To beautify as communicators, we have to not handiest research to speak efficiently, but additionally to pay attention with purpose. And, probably, if we exercising this diligently, we are able to uncover secrets in verbal exchange that had been formerly hidden in plain sight.

So, luxurious reader, are you ready to embark in this journey and get to the bottom of the mysteries of powerful verbal exchange? It's a journey that allows you to now not best help you reconnect together with your ex, however will even provide you with valuable device for all the relationships on your lifestyles. So take a deep breath and get ready to dive into the fantastic global of communication. And keep in mind: phrases are just the start.

If we consider communique as an art work, we understand that, like numerous artwork, it requires have a take a look at, exercising and, specially, authenticity. In fact, Deborah Tannen, in her ebook "You Just Don't Understand" (1990), addressed the complexity of verbal exchange among genders and the way our versions can reason misunderstandings. But past the phrases, what honestly subjects is the sensation, emotion and intention within the again of them.

Now, if we bypass from seeing verbal exchange as an artwork to seeing it as a technological know-how, we find captivating studies on how the thoughts processes statistics and the way our feelings have an effect at the way we talk. For instance, Dr. Albert Mehrabian, in his e-book "Silent Messages" (1971), proposed that high-quality 7% of communication is primarily based definitely on the terms we're saying, at the identical time as 38% is primarily based totally on tone of voice and fifty five% on body language. Surprising, isn't it?

But what does this suggest for you and your choice to reconnect? It manner which you have to be aware now not satisfactory of what you're pronouncing, however also the manner you are saying it. How commonly have you ever ever ever stated "I'm quality" with a tone or facial capabilities that actually suggests otherwise? Those are the moments at the same time as communique becomes greater than words. Those are the moments while our body, our tone and our emotions talk louder than any terms we are capable of utter.

And herein lies one of the satisfactory secrets and strategies of communique: consistency. When our terms, tone and frame language are aligned, we convey a clean and real message. But whilst they may be no longer, this is at the same time as misunderstandings arise.

However, statistics the concept is quality part of the puzzle. As George Bernard Shaw stated, "The hassle with communication is the illusion that it has taken area." So how can we make sure that our communique is effective?

The answer can also additionally lie in some thing as smooth as empathy. Empathy isn't certainly understanding what someone feels, however feeling it with you. And on the identical time as you talk with empathy, you are now not certainly speakme, you are connecting.

So, the following time you want to talk, ask yourself the following questions: What do I want to deliver? How do I experience about it? And how can I ensure that the opportunity character genuinely is acquainted with me?

The technique to those questions may not be on the spot, but with reflected image and workout, you could quickly recognize that effective communique is within your reap. Because, in any case, speaking isn't pretty masses speaking, it is about making people sense, recognize and, most importantly, be a part of.

To illustrate the power of communication beyond words, allow us to dive right into a concrete example, one that would resonate in many hearts.

Imagine Lucas and Valeria, a couple who, after years together, have reached a thing of stagnation in their relationship. They both enjoy that they now not "concentrate" to every outstanding. However, in the end, as Valeria modified into telling Lucas approximately a trouble at paintings, in desire to presenting answers or minimizing her problems as he normally did, Lucas in reality regarded her in the eye, nodded and said, "It need to be in truth difficult for you." That easy act, that acknowledgment, that 2nd of real listening and empathy, changed the tone of the complete communication.

But why did this easy gesture have the sort of profound effect? Dr. Brené Brown, in her paintings "Daring Greatly" (2012), highlights the significance of vulnerability in verbal exchange and the manner, by way of showing ourselves to be genuine and empathetic, we create deep and significant connections with others. Lucas failed to need to discover a way to Valeria's hassle; he genuinely had to be there for her, renowned her emotions and validate her experience.

On the opportunity hand, Dr. John Gottman, in "The Seven Principles for Making Marriage Work" (1999), talks about how ordinary gestures of connection, which includes a easy touch or a look, are vital to maintaining love and connection alive in a courting. It's about those seemingly small, however quite huge moments that remind us that we're on the same organization, that we care, and that we're inclined to understand and be understood.

And, speakme of facts and being understood, have you ever ever ever expert the disappointment of feeling that, irrespective of how hard you try to give an explanation for yourself, the opportunity character simply would not "get" what you are attempting to mention? Chances are, lots oldsters have felt this at one time or every different. But what if I advised you that the trouble isn't always in what we are saying, but in how we're pronouncing it?

Body language, tone of voice, choice of terms and, most importantly, the goal in the once more of our phrases, play a vital position in how our message is perceived. You may be saying "I love you," however if your frame language and tone do now not reflect it, your partner probable might not experience the equal manner.

So how can we ensure that our conversation is real and effective? It's approximately being present, being genuinely related to ourselves and to the opposite character, listening not excellent with our ears, but furthermore with our coronary coronary heart.

Perhaps, no matter the whole thing, the call of the game to powerful communique isn't so mystery. It's certainly approximately being right, real and present. Because, due to the reality the well-known pronouncing goes, "People will overlook what you said, they'll overlook what you in all likelihood did, but they'll in no manner forget about the manner you made them experience." And you, how do you need to be remembered?

Let's dig a hint deeper, diving into the less explored corners of communication. In a international ruled thru manner of text messages, emojis and short replies, it could be stated that we have out of place the capability to speak correctly. But it is in those depths that we discover the hidden gems, techniques and truths which have stood the test of time.

Stephen R. Covey, in "The 7 Habits of Highly Effective People" (1989), shared the perception that, to be understood, we want to first apprehend. Empathic listening, or listening with the purpose to understand, is greater than a dependancy, it's far an paintings. It is the act of putting oneself inside the special man or woman's shoes, feeling and seeing the arena from their perspective. This form of communication goes past words. It is a dance of electricity, an exchange of souls, a mystical second in which people join on a degree that transcends the physical.

As we hold this journey, it's far vital to bear in mind the importance of pause. Yes, silence. That awkward pause that such lots of fear. But did you understand that it is in that silence that the maximum profound answer is regularly decided? Alan Watts, logician and author, in "The Art of Contemplation" (1972), indicates that it is inside the silence the various notes that actual music is residing. Similarly, in communication, it's far inside the silence among the phrases that we frequently find the internal maximum meaning.

Now, allow me ask you a query: How regularly have you ever stated some factor you probable did now not mean to say surely because of the fact you probably did no longer take a moment to reflect? Words, once spoken, cannot be taken returned. That's why the pause, that treasured 2nd of silence, may be your remarkable exceptional buddy in effective communication.

As we pass beforehand, undergo in mind moreover the concept that it is not usually what you are saying, however the manner you assert it. Dale Carnegie, in "How to Win Friends and Influence People" (1936), stresses the significance of speakme from the coronary heart, being genuine in our interactions and recognizing the intrinsic charge of all and sundry.

In quick, powerful conversation, past phrases, is a tapestry of techniques, intentions and conventional truths. It is a aggregate of listening, empathy, authenticity, pause and, most importantly, love and appreciate.

As I stop this bankruptcy, I want you to take this essence with you: Communication isn't always simply an act of transmission, it's miles an act of connection. I invite you, as you still float ahead on this journey of restoration and self-discovery, to use the ones gadget to create big connections, no longer quality along side your ex, but with all of the ones around you.

And now, get equipped. In the subsequent financial damage, we will dive into the wealthy tapestry of affection rituals from a while past. You'll be surprised to find out how historic practices can light up your route to reconnection. Until then!

Chapter 12: Ancient Love Rituals

Since time immemorial, love has been the fundamental axis of human lifestyles. Every way of life, each civilization, has had its very very own expressions and rituals dedicated to this effective feeling. But have you ever ever stopped to reflect onconsideration on what those ancient rituals can train us? What if there were secrets and techniques hidden in these practices that might offer you with a whole new mindset in your modern state of affairs?

It is not virtually hobby that drives us to discover the historical rituals of affection. It is the deep need for connection, for belonging, and for understanding our very own hearts and souls. In the tumult of current-day existence, we have moved some distance from severa those practices, but that does not propose they've got out of region their relevance. In fact, they will be greater relevant now than ever.

Have you ever pressured why, no matter all our generation and "connectedness," we enjoy greater disconnected than ever? In a international in which we are able to deliver a message to the other aspect of the planet in a second, why is it so hard to talk with the simplest we adore?

Perhaps the answer lies in how our ancestors approached love. They understood that love have become no longer best a passing feeling, but a determination, a dance, a rite. Love became sacred and grow to be celebrated with rituals that strengthened the connection amongst couples.

For the historic Greeks, for instance, love modified into no longer simply one emotion, but a panoply of different feelings. They said Eros (passionate love), Philia (love among pals), Storge (familial love) and Agape (unconditional love). By information the ones top notch components of love, we'd start to see our non-public relationship in a top notch moderate. Isn't that charming?

So, as you embark in this journey through the affection rituals of beyond civilizations, I invite you to accomplish that with an open mind and a inclined coronary heart. Perhaps, within the midst of these ancient practices, you may find out the name of the sport you've got got been seeking out to reconnect collectively together with your ex.

Ask your self this question as we glide earlier: If the ancients had rituals and ceremonies for each segment of love, have to no longer we, in our modern-day age, have as a minimum one ritual, one exercise, that allows us reconnect with the ones we have got have been given misplaced?

Follow alongside, brave reader, as we discover collectively the hidden gems of the statistics and lifestyle of affection. And who knows, possibly in these ancient rituals you could find out the important thing to reignite the spark for your relationship.

Rituals and ceremonies not most effective constitute love and connection among two people, but moreover act as a bridge the various winning and the beyond, connecting us with previous generations. Through the ones practices, we immerse ourselves in an ocean of facts and manner of lifestyles, permitting us to get right of entry to device which can enhance our contemporary-day relationships.

In historic China, as an example, marriage come to be considered a sacred union, and marriage ceremonies have been complicated activities concerning severa rituals, every with a selected because of this. One of the maximum interesting rituals is that of "cup-crossing wine." Couples drank wine from cups joined with the aid of the use of the use of a purple string, symbolizing their intertwined destiny. Imagine for a 2d sharing a comparable ritual alongside aspect your companion or ex-companion, acknowledging the bond you as soon as shared. Don't you keep in mind you studied rituals like this can act as a balm, recuperation wounds and rebuilding bridges?

Or keep in mind the love practices of ancient India. In the well-known textual content, the "Kama Sutra," now not simplest are intimacy techniques described, but the importance of romance, seduction and foreplay is burdened. The paintings of courtship and seduction had been taken into consideration important to a loving dating. Now, what when you have been to undertake some of the ones techniques and convey them into your cutting-edge existence? Perhaps, through the usage of reviving the ones acts of romance, you can rekindle the ardour and desire in a relationship that has out of place its luster.

Robert Moore, in his influential paintings "The Archetypes of Love" (1989), argues that via the use of manner of analyzing and know-how those historical practices, we are able to pick out preferred archetypes of love. These patterns, which have persisted throughout time and cultures, can provide us a compass, guiding us in our look for love and connection.

Have you stopped to consider how those rituals can also inform and enhance your non-public dating? After all, inside the occasion that they have got stood the check of time, shouldn't they've got some element to provide cutting-edge couples?

In addition, historic cultures offer no longer handiest rituals and practices, however additionally memories and myths about love. These tales, passed down from era to generation, frequently contain pearls of know-how about the character of love, preference and loss. And it's miles regularly in those memories that we find out reflections of our very very own hearts and relationships.

In the subsequent section, we're able to find out concrete examples of these rituals and what we are able to analyze from them. In the period in-between, I invite you to reflect on what you have got were given have a look at thus far. Are there any historical practices that stand out to you? Any that you feel is probably relevant for your modern-day-day situation? Keep those questions in thoughts as we hold our journey thru the mysteries of affection.

It is in reality fascinating how some practices and rituals may additionally appear arcane, however their underlying standards are as applicable today as they have been millennia in the past. Let's permit our minds to excursion a hint in addition again in time and place. Let's see, through tangible examples, how historic love rituals may be particularly applicable and enriching inside the current-day context.

Take, as an example, the Celtic way of existence of "handfasting" or "tying hands". In this ritual, the couple's palms had been joined with a rope or ribbon as they declared their vows to each one of a kind, symbolizing a bond of affection and self-control. It is the shape of clean, but deeply symbolic gesture. Imagine for a second taking a few quiet time collectively along side your associate, becoming a member of palms and reaffirming your feelings for every other. Could this practice provide a reflective pause, a 2d of actual connection in our busy contemporary lives?

Or bear in mind the African love dance of the Wodaabe tribe of Niger. During the every year Gerewol competition, guys dress up in extravagant costumes and makeup, performing hard dances and songs to have an effect on girls. While at the begin appearance it is able to look like fine a curious way of life, there's a few factor deep at its middle: the concept of attempt, of displaying your notable self within the name of affection and admiration. And isn't always that what many want in a courting? For their partner to take some time, to care sufficient to offer their pleasant.

And right here comes a honest extra charming instance: in some indigenous tribes in South America, on the identical time as people enjoy a struggle or anxiety, they take a seat for the duration of from every different and percent a mate (a traditional drink). Without phrases, they simply drink collectively, passing the mate from one to the opposite. It is an act of sharing, a second of connection, wherein words are frequently superfluous. While it may look like a simplistic solution to modern troubles, isn't always the easy act of being gift and sharing a 2nd often step one to recovery and reconnecting?

The Art of Love: From Ovid to the Present Day" (2002) thru Michael Davis, factors out that notwithstanding the fact that times alternate and societies evolve, there are widespread truths approximately love that persist. Often, those truths are hidden inside the traditions and rituals we have inherited from our ancestors.

So now, luxurious reader, are you capable of see how, by means of using searching for to the past, we might locate the device to assemble a extra loving future? Can you note your self incorporating a few ritual or exercising into your life, adapting it for your present day context? What if I suggested you that the subsequent financial disaster will immerse you even similarly inside the technology of affection, supplying a fascinating counterpoint to the ones ancient traditions? But earlier than we keep, I invite you to mirror on the practices we have cited. Perhaps you may locate in them a course to a deeper know-how of affection and connection for your very very very own existence.

Now, as we dig deeper, we find out a recurring subject matter: the human choice for connection and expertise. It's clean to push aside rituals and traditions as relics of times past, however if we save you and surely observe their essence, we discover gemstones of facts. It is a reminder that, no matter the technology or lifestyle, the want for love and belonging is essential.

Take as an instance the historic Hindu ritual of Saptapadi, which is basically seven steps that the couple takes during the sacred hearth.

Each step symbolizes a vow, a choice for his or her lifestyles together. It is more than just an act of walking; it is a physical manifestation of their guarantees to each notable. And whilst it may seem far flung and uncommon to some, is not it basically what all people seeking out? Steps and guarantees, a shared route with a person we adore.

Stella Maris, in her artwork "Rituals of Love: Ancient Traditions in a Modern World" (1998), writes: "Rituals are a bridge among our internal self and the out of doors worldwide, an act that turns intangible love into something tangible." And he is right. Engaging in the ones rituals takes love from the vicinity of feelings to the arena of moves, solidifying its lifestyles in the actual worldwide.

But we need to not fall into the trap of seeing the ones rituals as magical solutions. It is not the act itself that includes the energy, but the motive inside the returned of it. It's the which means, the statistics, the dedication you supply to it that makes it precise. So as you check this, I invite you to expect: What rituals do you've got got have been given to your lifestyles? What acts do you perform, consciously or unconsciously, that provide a boost for your reference to others?

As we have were given journeyed together via these ancient practices, I hope you have got located, or rediscovered, the importance of symbolic gestures in love. Not handiest as a shape of expression, however additionally as a bridge to a deeper expertise of self and other.

To near this bankruptcy, I would like you to bear in mind some component critical. While it is beneficial to investigate from beyond traditions, love, in its essence, is everlasting and ever evolving. What topics isn't plenty the ritual itself, however the coronary coronary heart and sincerity with which it is carried out. In the following financial ruin, we are capable of dive into the captivating worldwide of neuroscience and discover how our brains way love. I promise it's far going to be an in addition enriching adventure Ready for the adventure?

Chapter 13: Neuroscience Of Love

It is charming how some factor as complicated and incomprehensible as love might also have roots in technological know-how. While emotions and emotions are summary, they have a totally actual and tangible domestic inner our anatomy: the thoughts. But have you ever ever ever ever stopped to consider what takes region in that organ even as you fall in love or while that love fades? Why can love be so intoxicating and, at the identical time, so devastating?

Neuroscience has provided revealing solutions to those questions that, for hundreds of years, have intrigued poets, philosophers and fans alike. Imagine for a 2nd if we may moreover want to enter the elaborate circuits of your mind and have a check, as spectators, the electric spectacle that takes place whilst you think of the one you love. Doesn't that sound like a thoughts-blowing adventure? Let me guide you via this adventure, wherein we are able to find out the secrets and strategies of the mind in love.

Have you ever harassed why, even as you fall in love, you sense butterflies in your stomach, your coronary heart beats faster and the vicinity appears brighter? It's no longer truly your imagination; it's far your thoughts freeing a series of chemical compounds that make you enjoy on top of the area. Dopamine, oxytocin, serotoninBut, proper here's some component curious to contemplate: did you know that the identical regions of the thoughts are activated as a whole lot at the same time as we experience romantic love as even as we take effective pills? That's proper! Love is actually like a drug for the mind. Would you dare to say that, in lots of methods, we become "addicted" to the individual we like?

While it is simple to immerse ourselves within the poetry of love, the real challenge lies in expertise the how and why. In the following sections, we're able to now not best find out the mysteries of the mind in love, but moreover discover how this effective tool adapts and adjustments at the same time as love fades.

Nature has a humorous manner of ensuring that, as a species, we preserve to breed and shape bonds. But what takes region at the same time as those bonds are broken? Why does the ache of a damaged coronary coronary heart enjoy so real and overwhelming? These are not actually rhetorical inquiries to get you questioning, they'll be questions that technological understanding has all began to reply.

Are you organized to delve deeper into the mysteries of love from a neuroscience mindset? I promise it'll be a journey for you to redecorate your information of love and equip you with knowledge which will serve you now not most effective to get your ex lower lower back, however to better recognize the very nature of human romance.

Let's delve a hint deeper into this fascinating universe of neurons and chemical substances. By studying the thoughts in love, researchers have recognized 3 number one tiers of love, each with its personal set of neurochemicals. Understanding those ranges will help you determine no longer only the motives in your feelings, however additionally the whys and wherefores of sure dating alternatives and behaviors.

The first stage is "Lust". Here, sex hormones, which incorporates testosterone and estrogen, take middle diploma. Remember those initial moments in a relationship in which the whole lot appears to revolve round choice? That overwhelming depth isn't always any accident.

Then, we bypass directly to the "Attraction" diploma. This is in which dopamine, norepinephrine and serotonin start to intervene. Helen Fisher, in her ebook "Why We Love: The Nature and Chemistry of Romantic Love" (2004), describes how those neurochemicals act as our mind's natural stimulants. That feeling of euphoria, strength and obsessive recognition on your accomplice? You can thank this trio of chemical materials for that.

The 0.33 degree is the "Union". Oxytocin and vasopressin are the celebs right right here. These are the chemical substances that, in principle, maintain us together prolonged enough to raise our youngsters. In "The Chemistry Between Us: Love, Sex, and the Science of Attraction" (2012) by way of manner of using Larry Young and Brian Alexander, how these chemical substances create that deep feeling of connection and dedication to a partner is explored.

But what takes location while the connection breaks up? It seems that the method of "falling out of love" additionally has its very own chemical cocktail. A decrease in oxytocin, the "cuddle" chemical, is idea to play a function within the feeling of disconnection. In addition, the strain of a breakup can growth ranges of cortisol, a strain-related hormone. And certain, it's far as ugly because it sounds.

So, looking at the neuroscience, it's far easy that we are not definitely on the mercy of invisible forces even as it comes to love. There are patterns, methods and, positive, even a sure predictability in how and why we fall inside and outside of affection.

With this clinical foundation, we have to argue that facts our brains can be a useful tool inside the technique of having an ex lower again or, no less than, statistics why we feel the manner we do after a breakup. And as we navigate this complicated neural landscape, it's miles crucial to don't forget that on the same time as our biology plays a role in our relationships, we are not intended to be slaves to our mind chemical materials. With know-how and know-how, comes the strength of choice and the capacity to chart our personal loving destiny.

Based at the above, permit me take you via a chain of concrete examples that illustrate the powerful impact of neuroscience on our love lives.

Imagine for a second Anna and David. The met at a bit occasion and felt a right away enchantment. During the primary few weeks in their relationship, Anna observed that she felt euphoric and complete of electricity, irrespective of the truth that she changed into slumbering lots less than famous. Her friends may want to inform her that she appeared to be "floating on a cloud." What Anna did not recognize on the time became that her brain become flooded with dopamine and norepinephrine, the chemicals associated with the attraction stage. All she knew turn out to be that she could not save you thinking about David, and on every occasion she received a message from him, her coronary coronary heart changed into pounding rapid and difficult.

Chapter 14: Understanding The Break Up

Break up is a complex way regarding many feelings and factors.

To begin the method of getting your ex again, you need to understand why the break up came about. This financial disaster makes a speciality of a complete understanding of the scenario.

Reflection on emotions

Start via thinking about your feelings. Understand the impact the cut up has had on you and renowned your ache and unhappiness.

This self-focus is vital for personal increase and lays the muse for a healthful method to reconciliation.

Find out why

Dig deep to find out the actual cause in the back of the breakup.

Was it due to relationship issues, insecurities, or outside pressures?

Understanding the muse motives is vital to growth powerful strategies to deal with and triumph over the ones troubles.

non-public growth evaluation

View the break up as an possibility for private increase.

Assess factors of your behavior and find out areas for development.

This introspection will now not most effective help you get your ex returned, however it's going to also assist your common nicely-being.

Analysis of relationship dynamics

Consider the dynamics of your dating.

What had been your strengths and weaknesses?

Understanding the patterns that induced the breakup will help you're making a plan for amazing alternate and specific your sincere preference to reconcile.

Make your intentions easy

Be smooth approximately your intentions.

Ask your self in case you need to get again together for the proper motives.

Don't looking for reconciliation due to loneliness or fear of being by myself.

Genuine purpose is important to a long-lasting and delightful relationship.

Looking for closure

In some instances, it may be essential to are searching for closure. This consists of having a deferential verbal exchange to understand your ex's mindset and feelings.

Closure permits us drift in advance and reconnect with a strong basis.

expert guidance

Consider searching out help from a therapist or relationship counselor.

A expert can offer treasured perception into your dating dynamics, offer coping strategies, and sell high-quality communique among you and your ex.

staying power of knowledge

Understanding that element is a method that takes time.

Patience is the key to resolving emotional issues and gaining clarity.

If you misunderstand the state of affairs and settle in haste, you could turn out to be repeating the identical mistake.

By making an investment the time and effort to recognize your cut up , you lay the foundation for a thoughtful and strategic approach to getting your ex again.

Give Yourself Time And Space

Emotions are raw after a breakup, and the temptation to make up proper away may be overwhelming.

But giving yourself time and place is an vital step in getting your ex lower back rapid and successfully.

emotional healing

Take the time you need to heal emotionally.

Breakup is difficult, and dashing to reconciliation without processing your feelings can prevent private growth.

Before repairing a courting, take time to grieve the loss and understand your own feelings.

Avoid impulsive conduct

Resist the urge to make impulsive alternatives.

Impulsive conduct together with sending emotional texts, calling regularly, or continuously harassing your ex can push him in addition. Give your self and your ex location to gain clarity and perspective at the state of affairs.

Self-contemplated image and personal growth

Use this time for self-expression and personal boom.

Identify your regions of development and actively paintings to end up the best version of you.

Not wonderful will this beautify your nicely-being, however it'll additionally display your ex which you are prepared for a effective change.

delimitation

Set clean obstacles together with your ex.

This consists of proscribing touch and keeping off conditions that aggravate emotional distress.

Boundaries create vicinity for non-public growth and prevent the continuation of terrible patterns that prompted divorce.

Rediscovering independence

Reconnect with factors of your lifestyles that would had been left in the back of within the route of your dating.

Pursue your interests, spend time with buddies and own family, and reputation in your private goals.

Rediscovering your independence will growth your vanity and beauty.

Break the addiction

If there are elements of addiction for your relationship, use this time to interrupt far from dangerous styles.

Builds self assure and independence.

This now not best contributes to private increase, but also lays the muse for balanced and sturdy relationships inside the future.

Insight and readability

Distance gives angle.

Take a step lower decrease lower back and objectively have a look at your courting and its dynamics.

This clarity is critical to information your and your ex-associate's roles in a divorce so you should make informed alternatives approximately your destiny.

Respect your ex's vicinity

Also, appreciate your ex's want for place.

Constant touching or making use of stress can make the pressure worse.

Give them the liberty to approach their emotions and make picks without being compelled or beaten.

The strength of now not something

It is actual that "absence makes the coronary coronary heart expand fonder." Power does now not permit both parties to miss each distinctive and understand the fantastic additives of the connection.

When controlled strategically, it creates a choice which could come to be a catalyst for reconciliation.

Set the reconnect timeline

Set an much less highly-priced time table for reconnecting. This does now not recommend you have to wait all the time, but you must have a plan for at the same time as and the manner you will reconnect. Setting an time desk will deliver your meeting a few structure and a enjoy of cause.

In end, giving your self time and region isn't always simplest a non-public need for healing, it's also a strategic step inside the tool of getting over your ex.

This lays the concept for a more mature, sturdy and bendy model and lays the premise for the following section of the manual.

Effective Communication

Communication is the foundation of any a achievement courting, and the use of powerful verbal exchange strategies is vital in case you need to get your ex again fast. This financial ruin explores the nuances of communication that foster knowledge, preserve in thoughts, and connection.

Open and sincere conversation

Have open and honest conversations.

Share your feelings, mind and thoughts about your dating with out guilt or blame. Create a vicinity wherein every you and your ex can explicit yourself with out worry of judgment.

active listening

Practice energetic listening.

Pay hobby to what your ex is pronouncing and try and understand their point of view. This indicates empathy and actual interest of their emotions and units the level for a sizeable trade of thoughts.

Avoid blame and accusations

Avoid accusations and blame.

Focus on expressing your feelings and reports in vicinity of pointing palms.

Create discussions that promote expertise in preference to developing protective reactions.

Using the "I" statement

Use "I" statements to specific your feelings and precise your troubles. For example, instead of saying "You normally sense horrible..." say "I revel in horrible...". This method creates a far less opposed surroundings and encourages fine talk.

time is of the essence

When starting an essential verbal exchange, endure in thoughts timing. Choose a time at the same time as each you and your ex are emotionally receptive and feature time to speak without interruption. Avoid touching sensitive topics even as emotions are immoderate.

recognize the boundaries

Respect your ex's barriers at a few stage within the conversation. If they want area or time to method data, deliver them the liberty. Pushing too difficult to discover a quick restore can create anxiety and avoid progress.

Admit it and express regret

Be prepared to admit your errors and apologize virtually.

Taking duty for your very personal movements indicates adulthood and a willingness to make first-rate changes. However, please be cautious as immoderate apologies can come across as insincere.

Focus on solutions

Shift your reputation from troubles to answers.

Work collectively at the side of your ex to discover first rate steps to move in advance.

Discuss how the 2 of you may help construct a healthy and awesome courting.

nonverbal communique

Recognize the significance of nonverbal conversation.

Pay hobby to frame movements, facial expressions and tone of voice.

Nonverbal alerts often deliver feelings that cannot be expressed in terms.

Setting verbal exchange desires

Set smooth verbal exchange dreams.

Be unique about what you choice to carry out through the verbal exchange, and ensure you and your ex are at the same net net page approximately those desires. This clarity offers course and reason to your efforts to reconnect.

Seek expert guidance

See a therapist or relationship counselor.

A independent zero.33 birthday celebration can facilitate verbal exchange, provide treasured information, and provide steerage in navigating complicated discussions.

Effective conversation is a dynamic approach that includes openness, empathy, and records.

Implementing the ones strategies will lay the foundation for rebuilding the traces of conversation and set the volume for the following steps in our manual on a way to get your ex decrease returned fast.

Chapter 15: Rebuilding Trust

Trust is a touchy element of a relationship, and rebuilding it after a breakup is essential to getting your ex decrease back rapid. This monetary wreck examines strategies for rebuilding broken accepts as proper with in a relationship or breakup.

Recognize keep in mind problems

Start thru acknowledging any believe troubles that could have contributed to the divorce. Identify unique activities or styles that broke the believe among you and your ex.

Understanding the inspiration motive is vital for effective solutions.

Systematic and sincere action

Restoring accept as true with calls for sustained and severe strive. Make a conscious try to maintain your promises and commitments. Small, massive gestures made constantly through the years can show agree with.

Expressing Your Thoughts Openly

Express your mind and feelings transparently and overtly.

Be open approximately your intentions and targets for the relationship. Transparency creates an ecosystem of honesty and lays the muse for rebuilding agree with.

Apologize and take duty

Offer a honest apology for any movements that would have contributed to the lack of acquire as proper with.

Accepting obligation for mistakes indicates a real preference to decorate and accurate.

Stop making excuses and interest on unique steps to enhance.

Set obstacles and expectancies

Set clear obstacles and expectations for the destiny.

Be clean about what you want from the connection and ask your ex what they want too. This mutual information helps save you future misunderstandings and will growth the sensation of safety.

Be affected person with the rebuild way

Rebuilding trust is a slow manner that requires patience.

Understand that take delivery of as actual with is constructed through the years thru regular and incredible actions.

Don't stress your ex to trust you right away.

Instead, popularity on showing your dedication through movements.

Transparency in communique

Ensuring transparency in conversation.

Be open about your feelings, mind and any difficulties you will be experiencing. This openness fosters vulnerability and authenticity and promotes the restoration of do not forget.

studies from past mistakes

Reflect for your past errors and actively artwork to look at from them.

Demonstrate your commitment to personal boom by means of using way of records the basis motives of accept as real with troubles and taking proactive steps to solve them.

Building emotional intimacy

Focus on constructing emotional intimacy.

Share your internal most mind and feelings along with your ex and encourage them to do the same. This emotional vulnerability fosters deeper connections and builds consider.

constant self-development

Strive for normal self-improvement.

Actively artwork to end up the amazing version of yourself with the resource of addressing the non-public problems that brought about the breakup.

This self-discipline to boom builds self notion on your capacity to exchange.

Rebuild accept as real with with moves, not phrases

Actions speak louder than phrases.

Show your commitment via concrete movements that healthful your terms.

If you generally display that you can trust your self, you may build greater take delivery of as real with than breaking our ensures.

counseling

Consider searching for help from a dating counselor or dating therapist.

A expert can provide tools and techniques to rebuild accept as true with, mediate conversations, and recognize dating dynamics.

In conclusion, rebuilding remember is a subtle but important approach.

By drawing near it simply, openly and patiently, you could lay the inspiration for a relationship built on a stable basis of believe and self perception, paving the way for a a fulfillment reunion collectively together with your ex.

Rediscovering Connection

Rebuilding your emotional connection is an important step in getting your ex yet again rapid. This financial disaster explores strategies and strategies for rediscovering the bonds that after existed and growing an surroundings wherein love and connection can flourish all over again.

Thinking of shared reminiscences

Think about the best and full-size recollections you shared.

Remember the moments that added you pride, laughter and connection.

This mirrored photograph permits create a pleasing emotional basis for repairing the connection.

expression of gratitude

Be thankful for the high-quality components of your dating.

Recognize your ex's functions and memories. This positivity creates an ecosystem of gratitude and reconnection.

Create new shared critiques

Create new recollections via using manner of introducing new shared reports.

Find activities or locations that interest you each.

Creating new recollections collectively strengthens emotional connections and allows cast off awful institutions from the past.

Quality time and presence

Prioritize nice time and recognition on the instant.

Whether it is a quick lunch, a stroll inside the park, or a weekend enjoy, spending uninterrupted time collectively can deepen your relationship. Put down your smartphone and simply have interaction inside the shared enjoy.

Vulnerability and authenticity

Be inclined and actual on your relationships.

Be open about your thoughts and emotions and encourage your ex to do the identical.

This vulnerability deepens emotional intimacy and strengthens emotions of accept as true with and connection.

A new appearance internal and jokes shared

Take a glance all over again at the internal jokes and shared jokes that have been a part of your courting.

Laughter has a powerful way of breaking down obstacles and developing a awesome mood.

Laughing together can rekindle the delight that added you together within the first place.

Actively pay attention and recognize

Learn to actively listen and try to recognize your ex's issue of view.

Express empathy and validate their emotions.

This builds a sturdy emotional connection through showing a actual interest in their emotions and critiques.

incredible gesture of affection

Impress your ex with a subtle gesture of love. It can be a handwritten take a look at, a small gift, or a gesture that shows your records of the opposite person's likes and dislikes.

A considerate surprise suggests your real care and trouble.

physical touch and intimacy

Gradually reintroduce bodily touch and intimacy.

Focus on respecting barriers and growing a sense of comfort and safety.

Physical contact plays an crucial function in restoring emotional bonds.

establishing mutual desires

Set goals for your relationship.

Discuss your vision for the destiny for my part and as a couple.

Mutual goal putting creates shared purpose and course and strengthens connections.

interest and participation

Learn the way to speak carefully.

Mindfulness manner being clearly immersed in the gift 2d without dwelling on the past or demanding approximately the future.

This presence improves the excellent of interaction and permits conversation.

Communication or remedy sports

Consider collaborating in accomplice sports activities or remedy.

Engaging in relationship-building sports activities or searching out expert steerage can provide you with the system and thoughts-set you need to enhance your conversation.

In quick, reconnecting manner accepting the excessive satisfactory factors of the beyond, developing new studies, and developing deep emotional connections. By intentionally nurturing the spark you as soon as had, you open the way to rekindling the relationship you as speedy as had.

Chapter 16: Facing Challenges

Relationships are often fraught with disturbing conditions, and navigating them is essential while trying to get your ex back rapid. This financial disaster explores techniques for coping with adversity maturely, locating commonplace floor, and not letting adversity stand in the way of reconciliation.

Expect and renowned challenges

Start through acknowledging that troubles are a herbal part of any relationship.

If you appearance ahead to this, you could resolve the trouble with a proactive method. Recognize that overcoming stressful situations can pork up and pork up your relationships.

maintain emotional manage

Learn a way to govern your emotions in the course of hard times. Avoid impulsive reactions and allow your feelings drift. Instead, take a step another time, breathe, and technique the scenario in a peaceful and composed way. Emotional balance contributes to optimistic trouble solving.

Communicate efficaciously while there are versions of opinion

Resolve variations of opinion thru effective verbal exchange.

Use "I" statements to calmly speak your thoughts and emotions and keep away from judgment. Encourage your ex to percentage their angle and actively pay attention and understand as opposed to react.

Find a common language

Identify not unusual and shared values.

In difficult instances, focusing on what you each agree on can be the muse of a solution. Understanding every other's middle beliefs can create a revel in of harmony although there are variations of opinion.

Search gives

We are open to good deal looking. Relationships frequently contain finding a middle ground that satisfies each companions.

Avoid a win-win mentality and as an opportunity art work collectively to find a answer that meets your and your ex's goals.

observe from beyond errors

Look decrease once more at beyond difficulties and errors and actively try to test from them.

Consider what patterns contributed to beyond problems and take proactive steps to interrupt the ones styles.

Demonstrating growth is vital to rebuilding take delivery of as real with.

Persevere irrespective of setbacks

Build resilience to conquer setbacks.

Not all reconciliation attempts pass with out problems and failure may additionally rise up.

Treat those setbacks as transient and no longer a reason to give up, but rather an possibility to reevaluate and enhance your approach.

Avoid the blame pastime

Avoid blame video video video games and finger pointing.

Instead of assigning faults, reputation on understanding the idea cause of the hassle. A no-blame method promotes a collaborative technique to hassle fixing.

Reflection and personal improvement

It encourages mirrored image and personal improvement.

Both you and your ex need to take duty for your very very own non-public growth.

Solving private troubles contributes to the overall fitness of your relationship.

encompass the alternate

Be open to alternate.

Recognize that overcoming a hassle regularly requires adjusting behavior, mind-set, or expectations.

Positive splendor of trade will foster the development of relationships.

Know while to trying to find out of doors assist

Recognize at the same time as you need out of doors help. If issues persist, are trying to find help from a relationship counselor or dating therapist.

Experts can offer facts, mild discussions, and provide gadget to address problems more efficaciously.

Consistency of notable behavior

Ensure consistency of superb conduct. Overcoming a problem is an ongoing system that requires ongoing attempt. Consistently demonstrating a willingness to make pleasant changes and face disturbing conditions will support your self-control to the relationship.

In stop, coping with adversity is an critical a part of dating repair. By drawing near traumatic situations with adulthood, effective conversation, and a determination to increase, you may pave the way for a more potent and additional harmonious bond collectively together with your ex.

Focusing On Self Love

In your efforts to get your ex decrease again speedy, specializing in self-love isn't always best crucial for your non-public happiness, but also performs an vital feature in rebuilding a wholesome and fine dating.

This financial ruin explores the significance of self-love, the way it influences the method of reconnection, and sensible strategies for fostering it.

Understanding Self Love

It begins offevolved with knowledge what self-love is.

This goes past superficial affirmation and indicates a deep appreciation and recognition of self. Recognize your well well worth, receive your strengths and weaknesses, and prioritize your happiness and achievement.

The dating among narcissism and courting fulfillment

Recognize the sturdy connection among self-love and relationship fulfillment.

When individuals love and contend with themselves, they devise high satisfactory and confident energy to relationships.

This in the end creates an appealing and first-rate dynamic for every partners.

Put your non-public properly-being first

Make your private properly-being your top precedence.

Participate in sports that convey you pride, improve your bodily and highbrow health, and make contributions in your standard well-being.

People who are happy and fulfilled have a more functionality to in reality have an impact on relationships.

Pursue your passions and pastimes

Rediscover and pursue your passions and hobbies.

Reconnecting with activities that supply you pride will now not first-rate boom your delight, but additionally make you greater exciting and dynamic as someone.

Setting and achieving personal goals

Set non-public desires and art work in the path of them.

Whether they will be associated with your career, private development or fitness, setting and conducting dreams offers you satisfaction and strengthens your capability to develop.

Create a useful resource tool

Surround your self with a manual network of buddies and family.

Having a strong help gadget gives emotional stimulation and reinforces the concept which you are really worth and loved even outdoor of a romantic dating.

Positive affirmations and mind-set change

Add tremendous affirmations in your each day lifestyles.

Resist negative self-speak and update it with affirmations that promote self-love and self-self perception.

Develop a mindset that acknowledges your definitely well worth and capability.

Practice self-care

Prioritize self-care practices.

This includes bodily self-care, which include exercising and healthful eating, further to intellectual and emotional self-care, which includes meditation and mindfulness.

Taking care of yourself as an entire contributes to a excessive outstanding self-image.

limits and rejection

Set healthful barriers and look at to say no at the same time as important.

Respecting obstacles and prioritizing goals builds shallowness.

This in turn promotes a healthy and balanced method to relationships.

Take a while for yourself

Take time for yourself as an possibility for self-discovery and growth.

Having amusing with yourself builds independence and self perception, trends that make a contribution to a strong and resilient individual.

www.ingramcontent.com/pod-product-compliance
Lightning Source LLC
Chambersburg PA
CBHW071441080526
44587CB00014B/1944